LODGINGS ALONG
THE APPALACHIAN TRAIL
IN
MAINE, NEW HAMPSHIRE, VERMONT, MASSACHUSETTS, AND CONNECTICUT

BY GARY KOCHER, Ed.D

APPALACHIAN TRAIL CONFERENCE

Cover illustration from 1858 lithograph entitled "Rockfish Gap and the Mountain House, Augusta Co., Va." from Edward Beyer's *Album of Virginia*.

Maps © 1989 by Country Roads, Inc., Orrington, Maine, H. Stacy Morin, cartographer

Published by the Appalachian Trail Conference
P.O. Box 807
Harpers Ferry, W.Va. 25425

© 1989 by Appalachian Trail Conference.
All rights reserved. No part of this book may be used or reproduced in any manner whatsoever without written permission except in the case of brief quotations embodied in critical articles and reviews.

First edition
Printed in the United States of America

ISBN 0-917953-35-5

The diamond Trail marker is a registered servicemark of the Appalachian Trail Conference.

TABLE OF CONTENTS

Introduction	i
Maine	1
New Hampshire	23
Vermont	47
Massachusetts	79
Connecticut	105

Introduction

Lodgings Along the Appalachian Trail is for hikers who wish to spend a weekend or more on the Trail without backpacking, but staying instead in accommodations off the Trail. To assist these hikers in planning their trips, the Appalachian Trail Conference has compiled information about motels, hotels, bed and breakfasts, country inns, cabins, hostels, and campgrounds (private and public) that welcome hikers and are within an hour's drive of the Trail.

HOW TO USE THIS BOOK

This edition of *Lodgings* covers the Trail area in New England (Maine, New Hampshire, Vermont, Massachusetts, and Connecticut).

It is divided by state, each chapter with a map showing the Trail, major roads, and the towns or cities where the lodgings are located. Each section also includes information on public transportation and shuttle services, access points to the Trail, and points of interest for each state. Appalachian Trail guides noted at the beginning of each chapter are available from the Appalachian Trail Conference, P.O. Box 807, Harpers Ferry, W. Va. 25425, (304) 535-6331. The trail clubs that maintain each section of Trail are also noted. Their addresses are also available from the Appalachian Trail Conference.

Accommodations are listed in chart form and divided into three categories: motels and hotels, bed and breakfasts and country inns, and campgrounds, cabins, and hostels. Each listing is divided into columns with the following headings:

Name and Address: Lodgings are listed alphabetically, first by town or city, then by the name of the lodging. If the mailing address is different from the actual location, the mailing address is in parentheses.

Telephone: Both local and toll-free numbers, if available, are given. If an establishment is not open all year, the season is noted.

Miles from Trail: Figures are provided by the establishment, in most instances.

Rates: Rates are rounded off to the nearest dollar. In most instances, the amount listed does not include taxes, and rates are subject to change at any time.

Credit Cards: Credit cards accepted by each establishment are indicated.

Food: Restaurants or carry-out lunches are noted as on premises, within a half mile, or farther with the mileage noted.

Office Open: The hours of the front desk or office are noted.

Park While Hiking: Most establishments will permit parking while hiking *for their patrons only*. Some charge a nominal fee. In all cases, be sure to secure manager's approval before leaving a vehicle.

Shuttle to Trail: Establishments that shuttle patrons to the Trail are noted.

Public Transportation: Public transportation to the facility or from the facility to the Trail is noted. (See "Getting There," at the beginning of each chapter, for more information. The lodgings should be able to provide phone numbers of taxi companies, if available.)

An explanation of codes appears at the bottom of each chart.

You may want to contact the establishments you are interested in and request brochures before your trip. They often have features that we did not have room on our chart to mention (for example, access to lake, beautiful views, *etc.*), and their brochures may help you decide. When calling for reservations or registering at any of the facilities listed, please identify yourself as an A.T. hiker and mention that you saw the listing in *Lodgings Along the Appalachian Trail*.

We based our information on answers supplied by the lodging establishments to questionnaires. Information herein was the most accurate available to the editors at the time of publication.

The Appalachian Trail Conference welcomes and encourages comments and suggestions from users of *Lodgings Along the Appalachian Trail*. Send all suggestions to Publications Department, Appalachian Trail Conference, P.O. Box 807, Harpers Ferry, W.Va. 25425.

The following people contributed to this book:

Nancy Mellert, coordinator
Ray Auger
Martin Beck
Neil Kenny
Stacy Morin
Reuben Rajala
Lois Scherer
Dorothy Wisniewski
Kay Wood
Rudolf Yondorf

MAINE

KATAHDIN TO MAINE-NEW HAMPSHIRE STATE LINE

Guide to the Appalachian Trail in Maine

The maintaining clubs for this area are the Maine Appalachian Trail Club and Appalachian Mountain Club.

GETTING THERE

Air: Scheduled service is available to Augusta, Bangor, and Waterville. Float planes that transport hikers to bodies of water along the Trail are available in some areas; check at airports in Old Town, Greenville, and Millinocket.
Bus: There is no service directly to the Trail. Cyr Bus Line has a daily run between Bangor and Caribou that roughly parallels the Trail; the nearest stop is at Medway, about 30 miles from Baxter State Park. A Greyhound route roughly parallels the Trail between Bangor and Portland. The nearest stop is at Newport, about 40 miles from Monson. Vermont Transit has a daily run between Portland and Burlington, Vt., which stops at Bridgton, about 50 miles from the Trail at Maine 26.
Taxi: Millinocket, Rangeley, and Rumford have taxi companies. Many small towns have informal taxi services. The chamber of commerce or postmaster in these towns can provide information: Bethel, Farmington, Greenville, Guilford, Milo, and Skowhegan.
Hiker Shuttle Services: Ken Hoyt, P.O. Box 105, Bryant Pond, Maine 04219, (207) 665-2460; Keith Shaw, Shaw's Boarding House, Pleasant St., Monson, Maine 04464, (207) 997-3597.

POINTS OF INTEREST

Katahdin: At 5,267 feet, the highest mountain in Maine is a worthy northern terminus for the Trail. The flora and fauna are similar to that found in the Canadian tundra, and the view is restricted only by the weather. The Trail to the summit is strenuous and exciting. The summit is five miles from the campground road in Baxter State Park.

Gulf Hagas area: North from the St. Regis Road, the Trail enters this area of striking, varied beauty. In less than a mile, the Trail reaches the center of the Hermitage, a stand of towering white "king" pines. Along the six-mile hike to the semiopen summit of Gulf Hagas Mountain are brooks and the remains of old lumbering operations. Most of the climb is not steep. Popular side trails lead to the gulf itself, a canyon with precipitous cliffs, waterfalls, and interesting rock formations.

Last link of the Appalachian Trail: Between Caribou Pond Road and the crest of Spaulding Mountain is a plaque commemorating the completion here of the last link of the Trail on August 14, 1937. The hike south from the road is about three miles and steep, but the views are rewarding. A one-mile side trail leads from this site to the summit of Sugarloaf (4,237 feet), Maine's second-highest mountain.

Saddleback Mountain: This five-mile hike north from Maine 4 is one of the most interesting and enjoyable in the state. The 4,116-foot summit is above tree line and has beautiful views. Along the way are unusual rock features, three small ponds, and strenuous climbing.

Mahoosuc Notch: The mile through the notch (about seven miles south of Maine 26) is billed as one of the most difficult stretches on the Trail. The notch is a deep cleft clogged with boulders and surrounded by sheer granite walls. Packs must be removed a few times to scramble under boulders and through small caves. The scenery is spectacular.

ACCESS POINTS

Parking is available at the Trail's road crossings. The Trail crosses gravel roads in Baxter State Park in Katahdin Stream Campground and Daicey Pond Campground (ample parking near Trail in park), Golden Road, a road from Nahmakanta Lake, Church Pond Road, B Pond Road, West Branch Pond Road (the previous four roads are all private, owned by the North Maine Woods Association, and may have tolls), St. Regis Road (private, seasonal), Long Pond Stream Tote Road, Elliotsville Road (limited parking), Maine 6/15, Shirley Road (limited), Moxie Pond Road (Trail follows it a short distance), local roads in the Caratunk area (some used by the Trail; many places to park), U.S. 201, a gravel road from Wyman Lake, a gravel road from East Carry Pond, Long Falls Dam Road, Bog Brook Road, East Flagstaff Road, Stratton Brook Road (the previous four are all gravel and may be closed in winter; limited parking along Stratton Brook and Long Falls Dam roads), Maine 16/27, Caribou Pond Road (also called Caribou Valley Road), Maine 4 (difficult to park here), Maine 17, South Arm Road, East B Hill Road, and Maine 26. Most lodgings will allow patrons to park vehicles on their grounds while hiking (see the "Park While Hiking" column in the listings).

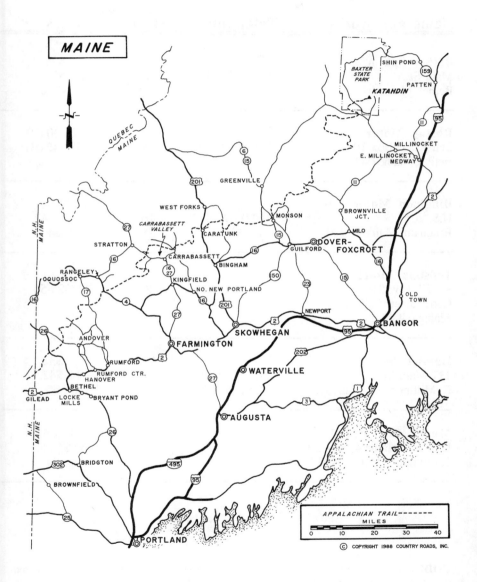

Maine

MOTELS AND HOTELS

Name and Address	Telephone	Miles from Trail	Rates
Bethel Spa Motel Main St. Bethel, Maine 04217	(207) 824-2989	20	sgl: $24 dbl: $34 xp: $10,c
Rostay Motor Inn Star Rt. 2, Box 101 Bethel, Maine 04217	(207) 824-3111	15	sgl: $25-30 (B) dbl: $38-42 (B) xp: $8,s,c
Bingham Motor Inn U.S. 201 Bingham, Maine 04920	(207) 672-4135	16	sgl: $26-41 dbl: $29-47 xp: $4
Judsons Motel Rt. 27, Box 2150 Carrabassett Valley, Maine 04947	(207) 235-2641	8	dbl: $25-50 s,c
Hamlet Motel 117 Main St. E. Millinocket, Maine 04430	(207) 746-5300 (207) 746-9030	30	sgl: $32 dbl: $42 xp: $5
Mount Blue Motel U.S. 2 & Maine 4, Box 5060 Farmington, Maine 04938	(207) 778-6004	30	sgl: $36 dbl: $40-50 xp: $4

CODES: sgl-single, **dbl**-double, **g**-group rates, **c**-special rates for children, **s**-senior citizen discount, **xp**-extra person, **MAP**-Modified American Plan, **AP**-American Plan, **B**-breakfast included, **V**-VISA, **MC**-MasterCard, **AE**-American Express, **CB**-Carte Blanche, **DC**-Diners

Credit Cards	Food	Office Open	Park While Hiking	Shuttle to Trail	Public Transportation
V/MC/AE	R L	7am-10pm	Yes	–	–
V/MC/AE	R-1.5 L	24 hrs.	Yes	–	–
V/MC/AE	R	until 10pm	Yes	Yes $5	--
V/MC/AE D	R-OP L	7am-1am	Yes	–	–
V/MC	R-OP L-OP	6am-midnight	Yes	–	–
V/MC/AE D	R L	7:30am-11pm	Yes	–	–

Club, **AM**-Amoco, **D**-Discover, **C**-Choice, **R**-restaurant within half mile unless mileage noted, **L**-takeout lunch within half mile unless mileage noted, **OP**-on premises, **E**-public transportation to establishment, **T**-public transportation to Trail, **n/c**-no charge

MOTELS AND HOTELS

Name and Address	Telephone	Miles from Trail	Rates
Evans Notch Motel U.S. 2 & Maine 113 RFD 2, Box 1245 Gilead, Maine 04217	(207) 836-2300	5	dbl: $40 and up
Big Squaw Mountain Resort Maine 15, P.O. Box D Greenville, Maine 04441	(207) 695-2272	20	sgl: $30-58 dbl: $30-58 xp: $12,s,c,g
Covered Bridge Motel (RD 2, Box 329 Dover-Foxcroft, Maine 04426) Maine 15, Guilford, Maine	(207) 564-2204	15	sgl: $30 dbl: $38 xp: $2,c
Farley's Motel Maine 157 Medway, Maine 04460	(207) 746-5162	20	sgl: $28 dbl: $38 s,c
Atrium Inn & Health Club Central St. Millinocket, Maine 04462	(207) 723-4555	20	sgl: $55-65 dbl: $65-75 xp: $5,c,g
Heritage Motor Inn 935 Central St. Millinocket, Maine 04416	(207) 723-9777	20	sgl: $60 dbl: $70 xp: $6,s,c,g

CODES: sgl-single, **dbl**-double, **g**-group rates, **c**-special rates for children, **s**-senior citizen discount, **xp**-extra person, **MAP**-Modified American Plan, **AP**-American Plan, **B**-breakfast included, **V**-VISA, **MC**-MasterCard, **AE**-American Express, **CB**-Carte Blanche, **DC**-Diners

Credit Cards	Food	Office Open	Park While Hiking	Shuttle to Trail	Public Transportation
V/MC	R L	8am-10pm	–	–	–
V/MC/AE	R-OP L-OP	24 hrs.	Yes	Yes $.55/mile	–
V/MC	R-OP L-OP	24 hrs.	Yes	–	–
V/MC/AE	R L	24 hrs.	Yes	–	–
V/MC/AE CB/DC/D	R L	24 hrs.	Yes	–	–
V/MC/AE D	R-OP L-OP	24 hrs.	Yes	–	–

Club, **AM**-Amoco, **D**-Discover, **C**-Choice, **R**-restaurant within half mile unless mileage noted, **L**-takeout lunch within half mile unless mileage noted, **OP**-on premises, **E**-public transportation to establishment, **T**-public transportation to Trail, **n/c**-no charge

MOTELS AND HOTELS

Name and Address	Telephone	Miles from Trail	Rates
Pamola Motor Lodge 73 Central St. Millinocket, Maine 04462	(207) 723-9746	20	sgl: $46 dbl: $49 s,g
Saddleback Inn P.O. Box 944 Rangely, Maine 04970	(207) 864-3434	7	sgl: $40-53 dbl: $45-50 xp: $5,c
Blue Iris Motor Inn U.S. 2, P.O. Box 127 Rumford Center, Maine 04278	(207) 364-4495	18	sgl: $30 dbl: $38 xp: $7,s,c
Stratton Motel Main St. Stratton, Maine 04982	(207) 246-4171	5	sgl: $25 dbl: $25 xp: $5,s,c,g
Stratton Plaza Hotel Main St., P.O. Box 620 Stratton, Maine 04982	(207) 246-2000	5	sgl: $25 dbl: $25 xp: $5,c

BED AND BREAKFASTS AND COUNTRY

The Chapman Inn P.O. Box 206 Broad and Church Sts. Bethel, Maine 04217	(207) 824-2657	15	sgl: $25-55 (B) dbl: $50-65 (B)

CODES: sgl-single, **dbl**-double, **g**-group rates, **c**-special rates for children, **s**-senior citizen discount, **xp**-extra person, **MAP**-Modified American Plan, **AP**-American Plan, **B**-breakfast included, **V**-VISA, **MC**-MasterCard, **AE**-American Express, **CB**-Carte Blanche, **DC**-Diners

Credit Cards	Food	Office Open	Park While Hiking	Shuttle to Trail	Public Transportation
V/MC/D AM	R-OP L-OP	6am-1am	Yes	–	–
V/MC/AE	R-OP L-1	24 hrs.	Yes	Yes donation	–
V/MC/AE	R-3 L	24 hrs.	Yes	–	–
V/MC	R-OP L	6am-9pm	Yes	–	–
V/MC/AE	R-OP L-OP	7am-8pm	Yes	–	–

INNS

V/MC/AE	R L	24 hrs.	Yes	Yes	–

Club, **AM**-Amoco, **D**-Discover, **C**-Choice, **R**-restaurant within half mile unless mileage noted, **L**-takeout lunch within half mile unless mileage noted, **OP**-on premises, **E**-public transportation to establishment, **T**-public transportation to Trail, **n/c**-no charge

BED AND BREAKFASTS AND COUNTRY

Name and Address	Telephone	Miles from Trail	Rates
The Foothills Farm Country Inn RR 1, Box 598 Brownfield, Maine 04010	(207) 935-3799	12	sgl: $34 dbl: $38 xp: $5,s,c,g
The Foxcroft B&B 25 West Main St. Dover-Foxcroft, Maine 04426	(207) 564-7720	20	sgl: $25 (B) dbl: $40 (B)
Evergreen Lodge B&B HCR 76, Box 58 Greenville, Maine 04441	(207) 695-3241	15	sgl: $46 (B) dbl: $53-59 (B)
Greenville Inn P.O. Box 1194, Norris St. Greenville, Maine 04441	(207) 695-2206	20	sgl: $44-60 dbl: $48-65 xp: $10
The Trebor Inn Golda Court Guilford, Maine 04443	(207) 876-4070	13	sgl: $38 dbl: $55
The Herbert Inn Main St., Maine 27 Kingfield, Maine 04947	(207) 265-2000 (800) The-Herb	14	sgl: $38-40 dbl: $46-50 xp: $10,g
Oquossoc's Own B&B Rangeley Ave., P.O. Box 27 Oquossoc, Maine 04964	(207) 864-5584	10	sgl: $25 (B) dbl: $40 (B) xp: $15,g

CODES: sgl-single, **dbl**-double, **g**-group rates, **c**-special rates for children, **s**-senior citizen discount, **xp**-extra person, **MAP**-Modified American Plan, **AP**-American Plan, **B**-breakfast included, **V**-VISA, **MC**-MasterCard, **AE**-American Express, **CB**-Carte Blanche, **DC**-Diners

INNS

Credit Cards	Food	Office Open	Park While Hiking	Shuttle to Trail	Public Transportation
–	R-5 L	24 hrs.	Yes	Yes $5/person	–
V/MC	R L	24 hrs.	–	Yes	–
V/MC	R-OP	6am-10pm	Yes	–	–
V/MC	R-OP L	6:30am-midnight	Yes	Yes	–
V/MC	R L	8am-10pm	Yes	–	–
V/MC/AE CB/DC	R-OP L-OP	8am-10pm	Yes	Yes n/c	–
–	R-OP L-OP	24 hrs.	Yes	Yes $1	–

Club, **AM**-Amoco, **D**-Discover, **C**-Choice, **R**-restaurant within half mile unless mileage noted, **L**-takeout lunch within half mile unless mileage noted, **OP**-on premises, **E**-public transportation to establishment, **T**-public transportation to Trail, **n/c**-no charge

BED AND BREAKFASTS AND COUNTRY

Name and Address	Telephone	Miles from Trail	Rates
Mt. Chase Lodge RD 1, Box 281 Patten, Maine 04765	(207) 528-2183 (open May to Nov., Jan. to March)	50	$45/person (AP)
The Widow's Walk Box 150 Stratton, Maine 04982	(207) 246-6901 (open 12/26 to 4/14, and 5/26 to 10/14)	5	sgl: $15 winter rates higher

CAMPGROUNDS, CABINS, AND HOSTELS

Name and Address	Telephone	Miles from Trail	Rates
South Arm Campground South Arm Rd., Box 310 Andover, Maine 04216	(207) 784-3566 (207) 864-5575 (open 5/1 to 10/15)	5	dbl: $10-18 xp: $5
Lone Pine Camping Area Star Rt. Box 200 Bethel, Maine 04217	(207) 824-2554	12	sgl: $7 dbl: $8
Harrison's Pierce Pond Sporting Camps P.O. Box 315 Bingham, Maine 04920	(207) 243-2930 (open May through Oct.)	0.1	$50/person (AP) $15/person (B) c,g
Peaks-Kenny State Park RFD 1, Box 48K Dover-Foxcroft, Maine 04426	(207) 564-2003 (open 5/15 to 10/1)	35	$9/site

CODES: sgl-single, **dbl**-double, **g**-group rates, **c**-special rates for children, **s**-senior citizen discount, **xp**-extra person, **MAP**-Modified American Plan, **AP**-American Plan, **B**-breakfast included, **V**-VISA, **MC**-MasterCard, **AE**-American Express, **CB**-Carte Blanche, **DC**-Diners

INNS

Credit Cards	Food	Office Open	Park While Hiking	Shuttle to Trail	Public Transportation
V/MC	R-OP L-OP	8am-10pm	Yes	Yes	–
–	R	8am-11pm	–	–	–
–	L-OP	8am-11pm	Yes	–	–
–	–	24 hrs.	Yes	–	–
–	R-OP L-OP	7am-10pm	Yes	–	–
–	R-6 L-6	8am-10pm	Yes	–	–

Club, **AM**-Amoco, **D**-Discover, **C**-Choice, **R**-restaurant within half mile unless mileage noted, **L**-takeout lunch within half mile unless mileage noted, **OP**-on premises, **E**-public transportation to establishment, **T**-public transportation to Trail, **n/c**-no charge

CAMPGROUNDS, CABINS, AND HOSTELS

Name and Address	Telephone	Miles from Trail	Rates
NOR'40 Campground RFD 4, Box 5220 Farmington, Maine 04938	(207) 778-6096 (open 5/15 to 10/15)	25	dbl: $8 g
Frost Pond Camps & Campground HCR 76, Box 620 Greenville, Maine 04441	(207) 695-2821 (open May to Nov.)	20	$7/site $13-15/person (cabin) c,s
Little Lyford Ponds Camps P.O. Box 1269 Greenville, Maine 04441	(207) 695-2821	2.5	$65/person (AP) s,c,g
Spencer Pond Camps Star Rt. 76, Box 580 Greenville, Maine 04441	(207) 695-2821 (open 5/15 to 11/15)	30	$12/person c
West Branch Ponds Camp Box 35 Greenville, Maine 04441	(207) 695-2561 (open 5/1 to 10/1)	4	$38/person (AP) c
Stony Brook Recreation U.S. 2, HCR 61, Box 130 Hanover, Maine 04237	(207) 824-2836 (open Memorial Day to Columbus Day)	30	$5/site plus $2/person

CODES: **sgl**-single, **dbl**-double, **g**-group rates, **c**-special rates for children, **s**-senior citizen discount, **xp**-extra person, **MAP**-Modified American Plan, **AP**-American Plan, **B**-breakfast included, **V**-VISA, **MC**-MasterCard, **AE**-American Express, **CB**-Carte Blanche, **DC**-Diners

Credit Cards	Food	Office Open	Park While Hiking	Shuttle to Trail	Public Transportation
–	R L-1	9am-9pm	Yes	–	–
–	–	8am-9pm	Yes	–	–
–	R-OP L-OP	24 hrs.	Yes $10	–	–
–	R-13 L-13	6am-10pm	Yes	–	–
–	R-OP	6am-9pm	Yes	Yes $5	–
–	R L	8am-10pm	Yes	–	–

Club, **AM**-Amoco, **D**-Discover, **C**-Choice, **R**-restaurant within half mile unless mileage noted, **L**-takeout lunch within half mile unless mileage noted, **OP**-on premises, **E**-public transportation to establishment, **T**-public transportation to Trail, **n/c**-no charge

CAMPGROUNDS, CABINS, AND HOSTELS

Name and Address	Telephone	Miles from Trail	Rates
Littlefield Beaches Campground Maine 26 Locke Mills, Maine 04255	(207) 875-3290 (open 5/25 to 10/1)	30	$13/site (2 adults) xp: $2
Katahdin Area Camping P.O. Box HA, Maine 157 Medway, Maine 04460	(207) 746-9349	30	$10-14 $20-25 w/hookup
Pine Grove Campground & Cottages HCR 86, Box 107 Medway, Maine 04460	(207) 746-5172 (207) 746-5705 (open 5/20 to 10/1)	30	dbl: $12-14 xp: $3
Airport Cabins 181 Medway Rd. Millinocket, Maine 04462	(207) 723-5513 (open mid-May to mid-Sept.)	0.2	dbl: $35
Jo-Mary Lake Campground Box 329 Millinocket, Maine 04462	(207) 746-5512 (open 5/15 to 11/1)	4	sgl: $9 dbl: $9
Millinocket Lake Camp and Big Moose Inn Box 98 Millinocket, Maine 04462	(207) 723-8391	10	sgl: $23 dbl: $38 xp: $8,s,c,g

CODES: sgl-single, **dbl**-double, **g**-group rates, **c**-special rates for children, **s**-senior citizen discount, **xp**-extra person, **MAP**-Modified American Plan, **AP**-American Plan, **B**-breakfast included, **V**-VISA, **MC**-MasterCard, **AE**-American Express, **CB**-Carte Blanche, **DC**-Diners

Credit Cards	Food	Office Open	Park While Hiking	Shuttle to Trail	Public Transportation
V/MC	R-1 L-1	8am-9pm	Yes	–	–
V/MC	R	8am-9pm	Yes	–	E
V/MC	–	24 hrs.	Yes	–	–
–	R L	24 hrs.	Yes	–	–
–	R-15 L-OP	9-5pm 7-9pm	Yes	Yes	–
–	R-OP L-OP	24 hrs.	Yes	Yes	–

Club, **AM**-Amoco, **D**-Discover, **C**-Choice, **R**-restaurant within half mile unless mileage noted, **L**-takeout lunch within half mile unless mileage noted, **OP**-on premises, **E**-public transportation to establishment, **T**-public transportation to Trail, **n/c**-no charge

CAMPGROUNDS, CABINS, AND HOSTELS

Name and Address	Telephone	Miles from Trail	Rates
North Woods Wilderness Camps Pemadumcook Lake P.O. Box 59 Millinocket, Maine 04462	(207) 723-4140 (open 4/15 to 11/1)	0.5	sgl: $18 c,g
The Old Church Hostel Corner Wilkens-Hebron P.O. Box 291 Monson, Maine 04464	(207) 997-3691 (open May to Oct.)	4	$8/person (AYH-ATC mbr.) $11/person (non-mbr.)
Happy Horseshoe Campground HCR 68, Box 170 N. New Portland, Maine 04961	(207) 628-3471 (open Memorial Day to Labor Day)	10	sgl: $9-12
Mooselookmeguntic House Rt. 4, Carry Rd. P.O. Box 331 Oquossoc, Maine 04964	(207) 864-3627	7	$50-75/cabin
Matagamon Wilderness Campground Box 220, Rt. 159 Patten, Maine 04765	(207) 528-2448	40	dbl: $7 xp: $1,g

CODES: sgl-single, **dbl**-double, **g**-group rates, **c**-special rates for children, **s**-senior citizen discount, **xp**-extra person, **MAP**-Modified American Plan, **AP**-American Plan, **B**-breakfast included, **V**-VISA, **MC**-MasterCard, **AE**-American Express, **CB**-Carte Blanche, **DC**-Diners

Credit Cards	Food	Office Open	Park While Hiking	Shuttle to Trail	Public Transportation
–	R-OP L-OP	7am- 9pm	–	–	–
–	R L	8am- 10pm	Yes	–	–
V/MC	–	9am- 9:30pm	Yes	–	–
–	R-1 L-1	8am- 5pm	–	–	–
–	R-15 L-OP	7am- 10pm	Yes	–	–

Club, **AM**-Amoco, **D**-Discover, **C**-Choice, **R**-restaurant within half mile unless mileage noted, **L**-takeout lunch within half mile unless mileage noted, **OP**-on premises, **E**-public transportation to establishment, **T**-public transportation to Trail, **n/c**-no charge

CAMPGROUNDS, CABINS, AND HOSTELS

Name and Address	Telephone	Miles from Trail	Rates
North Camps Hunter Cove Rd. Rangeley, Maine 04970	(207) 864-2247 (open Memorial Day to Nov.)	10	$45-75/cabin
The Terraces Housekeeping Cottages P.O. Box 3700, Rt. 4 Rangeley, Maine 04970	(207) 864-3771	8	dbl: $50 and up xp: $8
Cathedral Pines Campground P.O. Box 302 Stratton, Maine 04982	(207) 246-3491 (open 5/15 to 10/1)	10	$8-9/site $10-12 w/hookup
All Outdoors Troutdale Rd. West Forks, Maine 04985	(207) 663-2231 (open April to mid-Oct.)	8	sgl: $5

CODES: sgl-single, **dbl**-double, **g**-group rates, **c**-special rates for children, **s**-senior citizen discount, **xp**-extra person, **MAP**-Modified American Plan, **AP**-American Plan, **B**-breakfast included, **V**-VISA, **MC**-MasterCard, **AE**-American Express, **CB**-Carte Blanche, **DC**-Diners

Credit Cards	Food	Office Open	Park While Hiking	Shuttle to Trail	Public Transportation
V/MC	R-OP L-OP (May-June)	8am- 9pm	Yes	–	–
–	–	24 hrs.	–	–	–
–	R-2 L	9am- 5pm	Yes	–	–
V/MC	R-5	24 hrs.	Yes	–	–

Club, **AM**-Amoco, **D**-Discover, **C**-Choice, **R**-restaurant within half mile unless mileage noted, **L**-takeout lunch within half mile unless mileage noted, **OP**-on premises, **E**-public transportation to establishment, **T**-public transportation to Trail, **n/c**-no charge

NEW HAMPSHIRE

MAINE-NEW HAMPSHIRE STATE LINE TO CONNECTICUT RIVER

Appalachian Trail Guide to New Hampshire-Vermont

Maintaining clubs for this area are the Appalachian Mountain Club and the Dartmouth Outing Club.

GETTING THERE

Air: Scheduled service is available to Berlin and Lebanon.
Train: Amtrak stops at White River Junction, Vt. (about five miles from the Trail at Hanover), on a line between Washington, D.C., and Burlington, Vt.
Bus: Concord Trailways provides service directly to the Trail at Pinkham Notch daily on a line between Berlin and Boston, Mass., as does Vermont Transit to Hanover from Boston and New York City. Vermont Transit has a daily run through Crawford Notch on a line between Portland, Maine, and Burlington, but there is not a scheduled stop at the Trail crossing. The nearest scheduled stop is at the AMC Crawford Notch Hostel, about four miles north. Concord Trailways buses go through Franconia Notch on a line between Boston and Littleton and Colebrook, but there is not a scheduled stop at the Trail crossing. The nearest scheduled stop is at North Woodstock, about five miles south.
Taxi: Bartlett, Hanover, Holderness, Lebanon, Littleton, North Conway, Plymouth, and West Lebanon have taxi companies.
Hiker Shuttle Services: Ken Hoyt, P.O. Box 105, Bryant Pond, Maine 04219, (207) 665-2460. The Appalachian Mountain Club operates a scheduled shuttle service to Pinkham Notch, Crawford Notch, and Franconia Notch from several nearby towns, June to September. Write to AMC Hiker Shuttle Service, P.O. Box 298, Gorham, N.H. 03581, or call (603) 466-2727.

POINTS OF INTEREST

Mt. Washington: At 6,288 feet, this peak is the highest in the northeastern United States. The spectacular views from the summit on clear days are the centerpiece of a nearly 13-mile stretch of Trail above tree line in the scenic

Presidential Range. The mountain, originally proposed as the Trail's northern terminus, is noted for having "the worst weather in the world." The highest wind speed ever officially recorded on earth, 231 miles per hour, was registered at the summit observatory. The Trail to Mt. Washington is very steep and rugged from either north or south. The summit is about 13 miles south from Pinkham Notch (or 11 miles south from the intersection of the A.T. and the toll Mt. Washington Auto Road). Mt. Washington is 12 miles north of Crawford Notch.

Zealand Notch: The Trail follows the former roadbed of a nineteenth-century railroad, a reminder of the logging in the area at the turn of the century. In addition to relics of the logging and railroad history hidden in the woods, a boulder field gives testimony to the area's geologic history. The railroad bed begins about five miles south of Crawford Notch. Zealand Falls is about two and a half miles beyond. The Trail is steep and rugged in places.

Mt. Lafayette: At the 5,249-foot summit are the stone remains of a tourist building and views into the 18,560-acre Pemigewasset Wilderness. The peak is part of a two-mile stretch of Trail above tree line, with fragile alpine vegetation. The six-mile hike north from Franconia Notch to the summit is very steep and rugged.

Kinsman Mountain: Views from the twin open summits (4,358 feet and 4,293 feet, about a mile apart) are wonderful. Hikers pass scenic Lonesome Lake along the roughly six-mile climb south from Franconia Notch. The climb to the lake is moderate but is wet and steep after that. Hikers looking for a special challenge can then tackle the path down Kinsman Mountain, one of the steepest sections on the entire Trail. After reaching the secluded Harrington Pond, about a mile down, the shortest way to a road is back up.

ACCESS POINTS

The Trail crosses these roads, with parking availability noted: Hogan Road (parking lot), North Road, U.S. 2 (large parking lot), N.H. 16 (parking lot), the Mt. Washington Auto Road (a toll road; parking area at Trail crossing), U.S. 302 (small parking area; larger lot is just uphill on Wiley House Station Road, which the Trail follows), U.S. 3 (no parking at crossing, but one-mile Whitehouse Trail leads to large parking lot), N.H. 112 (small lot), N.H. 25 (difficult to park here), N.H. 25C (difficult), Atwell Hill Road (dirt), N.H. 25A (difficult), dirt roads in the Quinttown area, Lyme-Dorchester Road (which the Trail follows about one mile; small parking area), Goose Pond Road, Three Mile Road, Etna-Hanover Center Road, Dogford Road, and Trescott Road. The Trail also follows Sanitarium Road and a dirt Forest Service road in the Glencliff area (difficult parking on both) and several local streets in Hanover (several parking options). Most lodgings allow patrons to park vehicles on their grounds while hiking (see the "Park While Hiking" column in the listings).

MOTELS AND HOTELS

Name and Address	Telephone	Miles from Trail	Rates
The Lodge at Bretton Woods U.S. 302, Box SR Bretton Woods, N.H. 03575	(800) 258-0330 (in New Eng. ex. N.H.) (603) 278-1000	7	sgl: $65-95 dbl: $65-95 g
Mount Washington Hotel U.S. 302, Box SR Bretton Woods, N.H. 03575	(800) 258-0330 (in New Eng. ex. N.H.) (603) 278-1000	7	sgl: $105-235 (MAP) dbl: $170-340 (MAP) xp: $50
Tanglewood Motel & Cottages N.H. 16 Conway, N.H. 03818	(603) 447-5932	20	sgl: $46-53 dbl: $46-63 xp: $7,c
Gale River Motel 40 Main St. RFD 1, Box 153 Franconia, N.H. 03580	(603) 823-5655 (800) 255-7989	5	sgl: $49 dbl: $52-70 xp: $6
Best Western Storybook Resort Inn U.S. 302 and N.H. 16 Glen, N.H. 03838	(603) 383-6800	12	sgl: $59 dbl: $59-79 xp: $6,g
Linderhof Motor Inn Box 126, N.H. 16 Glen, N.H. 03838	(603) 383-4334	10	sgl: $28-69 dbl: $38-79 xp: $5,c,g

CODES: sgl-single, **dbl**-double, **g**-group rates, **c**-special rates for children, **s**-senior citizen discount, **xp**-extra person, **MAP**-Modified American Plan, **AP**-American Plan, **B**-breakfast included, **V**-VISA, **MC**-MasterCard, **AE**-American Express, **CB**-Carte Blanche, **DC**-Diners

Credit Cards	Food	Office Open	Park While Hiking	Shuttle to Trail	Public Transportation
V/MC/AE DC/D	R-OP L	24 hrs.	Yes	Yes	E T
V/MC/AE DC/D	R-OP L-OP	24 hrs.	Yes	Yes	E T
V/MC/AE	R L	8am-11pm	Yes	–	–
V/MC/AE D	R L	24 hrs.	Yes	–	–
all major	R-OP L	8am-midnight	Yes	–	E
V/MC/AE	R-OP	24 hrs.	Yes	–	–

Club, **AM**-Amoco, **D**-Discover, **C**-Choice, **R**-restaurant within half mile unless mileage noted, **L**-takeout lunch within half mile unless mileage noted, **OP**-on premises, **E**-public transportation to establishment, **T**-public transportation to Trail, **n/c**-no charge

New Hampshire

MOTELS AND HOTELS

Name and Address	Telephone	Miles from Trail	Rates
Mt. Madison Motel 365 Main St. Gorham, N.H. 03581	(603) 466-3622 (open 4/15 to 11/15)	3	sgl: $30-40 dbl: $40-50 xp: $5
Tourist Village Motel 130 Main St. Gorham, N.H. 03581	(603) 466-3312	3	sgl: $29-60 dbl: $34-64 xp: $5-6
Old Field House Hotel N.H. 16A Intervale, N.H. 03845	(603) 356-5478	12	sgl: $60-90 dbl: $60-90 xp: $10
Perrys Motel & Cottages N.H. 16A Intervale, N.H. 03845	(603) 356-2214 (open May-Oct.)	15	sgl: $20 dbl: $20 xp: $7,c
Swiss Chalets Motel N.H. 16A Intervale, N.H. 03845	(603) 356-2232	15	sgl: $45-69 dbl: $59-115 xp: $6
Covered Bridge Motor Lodge N.H. 16, Box V Jackson, N.H. 03846	(800) 634-2911 (603) 383-9151	10	sgl: $40-52 dbl: $44-70 xp: $10
Eagle Mountain House Carter Notch Rd. Jackson, N.H. 03846	(603) 383-9111	16	sgl: $60-150 dbl: $60-150 xp: $15

CODES: sgl-single, **dbl**-double, **g**-group rates, **c**-special rates for children, **s**-senior citizen discount, **xp**-extra person, **MAP**-Modified American Plan, **AP**-American Plan, **B**-breakfast included, **V**-VISA, **MC**-MasterCard, **AE**-American Express, **CB**-Carte Blanche, **DC**-Diners

Credit Cards	Food	Office Open	Park While Hiking	Shuttle to Trail	Public Transportation
V/MC/AE D	R L	24 hrs.	Yes	–	–
V/MC/AE D	R L	7am-11pm	Yes	–	–
V/MC/AE	R L-1.5	8am-10pm	Yes	–	–
–	R L-1.5	8:30am-8:30pm	Yes	–	–
V/MC	R L	7:30am-9:30pm	Yes	–	–
V/MC/AE	R	8am-midnight	Yes	–	E
V/MC/AE	R	24 hrs.	Yes	–	–

Club, **AM**-Amoco, **D**-Discover, **C**-Choice, **R**-restaurant within half mile unless mileage noted, **L**-takeout lunch within half mile unless mileage noted, **OP**-on premises, **E**-public transportation to establishment, **T**-public transportation to Trail, **n/c**-no charge

New Hampshire

MOTELS AND HOTELS

Name and Address	Telephone	Miles from Trail	Rates
Wentworth Resort Hotel N.H. 16A Jackson, N.H. 03846	(800) 637-0013 (in New Eng. ex. N.H.) (603) 383-9700	10	sgl: $75-135 dbl: $75-135 xp: $10
Evergreen Motel U.S. 2, P.O. Box 33 Jefferson, N.H. 03583	(603) 586-4449	10	sgl: $30-45 dbl: $32-48 xp: $5
Franconia Notch Motel RFD 1, Box 98B, U.S. 3 Lincoln, N.H. 03251	(603) 745-2229	2	sgl: $30-42 dbl: $32-55 xp: $5
Indian Head Resort U.S. 3 Lincoln, N.H. 03251	(603) 745-8000	1.5	dbl: $58-108 xp: $15
Parker's Motel U.S. 3 Lincoln, N.H. 03251	(603) 745-8341	1.5	sgl: $40-60 dbl: $50-70 xp: $5
Eastern Inns N.H. 16, P.O. Box 775 North Conway, N.H. 03860	(603) 356-5447	20	sgl: $45-66 dbl: $51-72 xp: $6,c
Fox Ridge Resort N.H. 16, P.O. Box 990 North Conway, N.H. 03860	(603) 356-3151	20	dbl: $85-130 xp: $6

CODES: **sgl**-single, **dbl**-double, **g**-group rates, **c**-special rates for children, **s**-senior citizen discount, **xp**-extra person, **MAP**-Modified American Plan, **AP**-American Plan, **B**-breakfast included, **V**-VISA, **MC**-MasterCard, **AE**-American Express, **CB**-Carte Blanche, **DC**-Diners

Credit Cards	Food	Office Open	Park While Hiking	Shuttle to Trail	Public Transportation
V/MC/AE	R-OP L-OP	24 hrs.	Yes	–	E
V/MC/AE	R-OP L-OP	24 hrs.	Yes	–	–
V/MC	R L	8am-11pm	Yes	–	–
all major	R-OP L-OP	7am-10pm	Yes	Yes	E
V/MC/AE D	R L-1.5	8am-10pm	Yes	Yes cost varies	–
V/MC/AE DC	R L	24 hrs.	Yes	–	E
V/MC	R-OP L	24 hrs.	Yes	-	-

Club, **AM**-Amoco, **D**-Discover, **C**-Choice, **R**-restaurant within half mile unless mileage noted, **L**-takeout lunch within half mile unless mileage noted, **OP**-on premises, **E**-public transportation to establishment, **T**-public transportation to Trail, **n/c**-no charge

MOTELS AND HOTELS

Name and Address	Telephone	Miles from Trail	Rates
Green Granite Motel and Conference Center N.H. 16, P.O. Box 3127 North Conway, N.H. 03860	(800) 468-3666 (603) 356-6901	20	dbl: $44-150 xp: $8,s,c
Merrill Farm Resort N.H. 16, RFD Box 151 North Conway, N.H. 03818	(800) 445-1017 (in New Eng. ex. N.H.) (603) 447-3866	20	sgl: $39-59 dbl: $39-79 xp: $10,s,c,g
Deep River Motor Inn Highland St., P.O. Box 95 Plymouth, N.H. 03264	(603) 536-2155	17	sgl: $37-45 dbl: $39-56 xp: $6,s
Pilgrim Motel RD 1 Plymouth, N.H. 03264	(603) 536-1319	25	sgl: $30 dbl: $38-42
Thrifty Yankee Lodge U.S. 3 Plymouth, N.H. 03264	(603) 536-2330	20	sgl: $30 dbl: $41-45 xp: $5
Grand View Lodge Rt. 2 Randolph, N.H. 03570	(603) 466-5715	2	sgl: $28 dbl: $44 xp: $6
Four Seasons Motor Inn U.S. 3 & Birch Rd. Twin Mtn., N.H. 03595	(800) 228-5708 (except N.H.) (603) 846-5708	20	sgl: $40 dbl: $60 xp: $5

CODES: sgl-single, **dbl**-double, **g**-group rates, **c**-special rates for children, **s**-senior citizen discount, **xp**-extra person, **MAP**-Modified American Plan, **AP**-American Plan, **B**-breakfast included, **V**-VISA, **MC**-MasterCard, **AE**-American Express, **CB**-Carte Blanche, **DC**-Diners

Credit Cards	Food	Office Open	Park While Hiking	Shuttle to Trail	Public Transportation
V/MC/AE	R L	24 hrs.	Yes	–	–
all major	R L	8am-10pm	Yes	–	E
V/MC	R-1 L	7am-11pm	Yes	Yes $10	–
V/MC	R L	8am-11pm	Yes	–	–
V/MC/AE D	R L	7am-11pm	–	–	–
V/MC/AE D	R-3 L-OP	8am-9pm	Yes	Yes	E
V/MC	R L	9am-10pm	Yes	–	–

Club, **AM**-Amoco, **D**-Discover, **C**-Choice, **R**-restaurant within half mile unless mileage noted, **L**-takeout lunch within half mile unless mileage noted, **OP**-on premises, **E**-public transportation to establishment, **T**-public transportation to Trail, **n/c**-no charge

MOTELS AND HOTELS

Name and Address	Telephone	Miles from Trail	Rates
Tamarack Motel and Cabins U.S. 302 Twin Mtn., N.H. 03595	(603) 846-5700	5	sgl: $35 dbl: $57
Wheelock Motor Court U.S. 3, P.O. Box E Woodstock, N.H. 03293	(603) 745-8771	10	sgl: $25-38 dbl: $35-42 xp: $5,c,g

BED AND BREAKFASTS AND COUNTRY

Name and Address	Telephone	Miles from Trail	Rates
The Bretton Arms Off U.S. 302 Bretton Woods, N.H. 03575	(800) 258-0330 (New Eng. ex. N.H.) (603) 278-1000	7	sgl: $125-135 dbl: $125-135 xp: $15,c,g
The Darby Field Inn Bald Hill, P.O. Box D Conway, N.H. 03818	(603) 447-2181 (open May to early Nov. and mid-Nov. to April)	20	sgl: $90 (MAP), $75 (B) dbl: $140 (MAP), $110 (B) xp: $40,c
Blanche's B&B N.H. 116, Easton Valley Rd. RFD 1, Box 75 Franconia, N.H. 03580	(603) 823-7061	6	sgl: $35 (B) dbl: $50 (B) xp: $20

CODES: sgl-single, **dbl**-double, **g**-group rates, **c**-special rates for children, **s**-senior citizen discount, **xp**-extra person, **MAP**-Modified American Plan, **AP**-American Plan, **B**-breakfast included, **V**-VISA, **MC**-MasterCard, **AE**-American Express, **CB**-Carte Blanche, **DC**-Diners

Credit Cards	Food	Office Open	Park While Hiking	Shuttle to Trail	Public Transportation
V/MC/AE CB/D	R L	7am-10pm	–	–	–
V/MC/AE D	R-5 L-1	24 hrs.	Yes	–	–

INNS

Credit Cards	Food	Office Open	Park While Hiking	Shuttle to Trail	Public Transportation
V/MC/AE DC/D	R-OP L-OP	24 hrs.	Yes	Yes	E T
V/MC/AE	R-OP L-2.5	9am-9pm	–	Yes	–
V/MC	R-3 L-3	8am-10pm	Yes	–	–

Club, **AM**-Amoco, **D**-Discover, **C**-Choice, **R**-restaurant within half mile unless mileage noted, **L**-takeout lunch within half mile unless mileage noted, **OP**-on premises, **E**-public transportation to establishment, **T**-public transportation to Trail, **n/c**-no charge

BED AND BREAKFASTS AND COUNTRY

Name and Address	Telephone	Miles from Trail	Rates
Bungay Jar B&B P.O. Box 15 Easton Valley Rd. Franconia, N.H. 03580	(603) 823-7775	1.5	sgl: $45 (B) dbl: $55 (B) xp: $20
Franconia Inn Easton Rd., N.H. 116 Franconia, N.H. 03580	(603) 823-5542 (open 5/31 to 11/1 and 12/15 to 4/1)	3	sgl: $90 (MAP) dbl: $130 (MAP) xp: $38,c,g
The Red Apple Inn U.S. 302 Glen, N.H. 03838	(603) 383-9680	14	dbl: $33-69 xp: $5
The Gables 139 Main St. Gorham, N.H. 03581	(603) 466-2876 (open Jan. to Oct.)	2.5	sgl: $25-30 (B) dbl: $45-50 (B)
Moose Mountain Lodge Box 272 Etna, N.H. 03750	(603) 643-3529 (open 6/1 to 11/1 and 12/26 to 3/21)	2	sgl: $74 (MAP) dbl: $128 (MAP) xp: $59, hiker disc.,c,s,g
Haverhill Inn N.H. 10, Box 95 Haverhill, N.H. 03765	(603) 989-5961	10	sgl: $35-50 (B) dbl: $65 (B) xp: $15
Wildcat Inn and Tavern Main St., P.O. Box T Jackson, N.H. 03846	(603) 383-4216	7	sgl: $40 (B) dbl: $60-68 (B) dbl: $100 (MAP)

CODES: sgl-single, **dbl**-double, **g**-group rates, **c**-special rates for children, **s**-senior citizen discount, **xp**-extra person, **MAP**-Modified American Plan, **AP**-American Plan, **B**-breakfast included, **V**-VISA, **MC**-MasterCard, **AE**-American Express, **CB**-Carte Blanche, **DC**-Diners

INNS

Credit Cards	Food	Office Open	Park While Hiking	Shuttle to Trail	Public Transportation
AE	R-2.5 L-OP	8am- 10pm	Yes	Yes	–
V/MC/AE	R-OP L-OP	8am- 10pm	Yes	Yes $10/person	–
V/MC/AE	R L	7:30am- 10pm	Yes	–	–
AE	R L	8am- 10pm	Yes	–	E T
V/MC	R-OP L-OP	7:30am- 9pm	Yes	Yes n/c	–
–	R-5 L-4	8am- 10pm	Yes	Yes n/c	–
V/MC/AE	R-OP L-OP	7am- midnight	Yes	–	E

Club, **AM**-Amoco, **D**-Discover, **C**-Choice, **R**-restaurant within half mile unless mileage noted, **L**-takeout lunch within half mile unless mileage noted, **OP**-on premises, **E**-public transportation to establishment, **T**-public transportation to Trail, **n/c**-no charge

BED AND BREAKFASTS AND COUNTRY

Name and Address	Telephone	Miles from Trail	Rates
The Lyme Inn On the Common Lyme, N.H. 03768	(603) 795-2222	5	sgl: $77-83 (MAP) dbl: $116-150 (MAP) xp: $35
Cranmore Mtn. Lodge Kearsarge Rd., P.O. Box 1194 North Conway, N.H. 03860	(603) 356-2044	20	sgl: $24 (dorm) (B) dbl: $65-105 (B) xp: $10-25,c,g
Nereledge Inn River Rd. North Conway, N.H. 03860	(603) 356-2831	25	sgl: $40 dbl: $55 xp: $15
Sunnyside Inn Seavey St. North Conway, N.H. 03860	(603) 356-6239	15	sgl: $24 (B) dbl: $34-58 (B) xp: $15,c,g
The Birches B&B Rt. 175 North Woodstock, N.H. 03262	(603) 745-6603	6	sgl: $45-50 (B) dbl: $60-70 (B) xp: $25,c
The Cascade Lodge U.S. 3, Main St., P.O Box 95 North Woodstock, N.H. 03262	(603) 745-2722	9	sgl: $17 (B)
The Woodstock Inn P.O. Box 118, U.S. 3 North Woodstock, N.H. 03262	(603) 745-3951	8	sgl: $45-69 dbl: $58-79 xp: $15,c

CODES: sgl-single, **dbl**-double, **g**-group rates, **c**-special rates for children, **s**-senior citizen discount, **xp**-extra person, **MAP**-Modified American Plan, **AP**-American Plan, **B**-breakfast included, **V**-VISA, **MC**-MasterCard, **AE**-American Express, **CB**-Carte Blanche, **DC**-Diners

INNS

Credit Cards	Food	Office Open	Park While Hiking	Shuttle to Trail	Public Transportation
V/MC/AE	R-OP L	8am-10pm	Yes	–	E
V/MC/AE D	R-OP L-OP	7am-11pm	Yes	–	E
V/MC/AE	R L-OP	24 hrs.	Yes	Yes	E
V/MC	R L	24 hrs.	Yes	Yes n/c	E
–	R-1 L-1	7am-9pm	Yes	–	–
AE	R L	8am-10pm	Yes	Yes	–
V/MC/AE DC	R-OP L-OP	8am-11pm	Yes	–	–

Club, **AM**-Amoco, **D**-Discover, **C**-Choice, **R**-restaurant within half mile unless mileage noted, **L**-takeout lunch within half mile unless mileage noted, **OP**-on premises, **E**-public transportation to establishment, **T**-public transportation to Trail, **n/c**-no charge

BED AND BREAKFASTS AND COUNTRY

Name and Address	Telephone	Miles from Trail	Rates
The Hilltop Inn N.H. 117, Main St. Sugar Hill, N.H. 03585	(603) 823-5695	7	sgl: $40 and up (B) dbl: $50 and up (B) xp: $10,c,g
Ledgelands Inn & Cottages RR 1, Box 94 Sugar Hill, N.H. 03585	(603) 823-5341	8	sgl: $38-100 dbl: $56-100 xp: $16,g
The Black Iris S. Main St., P.O. Box 83 Warren, N.H. 03279	(603) 764-9366	8	sgl: $30-40 dbl: $40-50 xp: $15,c
Wentworth Inn & Art Gallery Ellsworth Hill Rd. Wentworth, N.H. 03282	(603) 764-9923 (800) 542-2331	10	sgl: $45 dbl: $55-75 xp: $15,g
Kimball Hill Inn P.O. Box 74, Kimball Hill Rd. Whitefield, N.H. 03598	(603) 837-2284	15	sgl: $35-65 dbl: $35-65 xp: $5

CODES: sgl-single, **dbl**-double, **g**-group rates, **c**-special rates for children, **s**-senior citizen discount, **xp**-extra person, **MAP**-Modified American Plan, **AP**-American Plan, **B**-breakfast included, **V**-VISA, **MC**-MasterCard, **AE**-American Express, **CB**-Carte Blanche, **DC**-Diners

INNS

Credit Cards	Food	Office Open	Park While Hiking	Shuttle to Trail	Public Transportation
V/MC/AE	R-2.5 L-2.5	7am-11pm	Yes	Yes n/c	E
–	R L-2	7am-9pm	Yes	–	–
–	R L-OP	after 5pm weekdays, all day weekends	Yes	Yes	–
V/MC/AE DC	R-OP L-OP	9am-8pm	Yes	–	–
V/MC/AE	R-1.5 L-1.5	8am-8pm	Yes	Yes $5	–

Club, **AM**-Amoco, **D**-Discover, **C**-Choice, **R**-restaurant within half mile unless mileage noted, **L**-takeout lunch within half mile unless mileage noted, **OP**-on premises, **E**-public transportation to establishment, **T**-public transportation to Trail, **n/c**-no charge

New Hampshire

CAMPGROUNDS, CABINS, AND HOSTELS

Name and Address	Telephone	Miles from Trail	Rates
Moose Brook State Park RR 1, 30 Jimtown Rd. Berlin, N.H. 03570	(603) 466-3860 (open late May to Labor Day)	6	$10/site c
Apple Hill Campground N.H. 142 N, P.O. Box 388 Bethlehem, N.H. 03574	(603) 869-2238	12	dbl: $11-13 xp: $2,c,g
Crescent Campsites Fernwood Farm Rd. P.O. Box 238 Canaan, N.H. 03741	(603) 523-9910 (open 5/15 to 10/15)	15	$11-14/site xp: $1,c,g
Lafayette Place Campground Franconia Notch State Park Franconia, N.H. 03580	(603) 823-5563	2.5	$10/site
Green Meadow Camp Area N.H. 16, P.O. Box 246 Glen, N.H. 03838	(603) 383-6801 (Memorial Day weekend to Columbus Day weekend)	10	$13 w/hook-up $11 without xp: $2
Pinkham Notch Camp P.O. Box 298, N.H. 16 Gorham, N.H. 03581	(603) 466-2727 reserv. necessary	on Trail	sgl: $27-35 (inc. meals) c, AMC mbr. disc.

CODES: sgl-single, **dbl**-double, **g**-group rates, **c**-special rates for children, **s**-senior citizen discount, **xp**-extra person, **MAP**-Modified American Plan, **AP**-American Plan, **B**-breakfast included, **V**-VISA, **MC**-MasterCard, **AE**-American Express, **CB**-Carte Blanche, **DC**-Diners

Credit Cards	Food	Office Open	Park While Hiking	Shuttle to Trail	Public Transportation
–	R-1.5 L-2	9am-9pm	Yes	–	–
–	R L-1	8am-10pm	Yes	–	E
–	R-2 L-2	9:30am-9pm	Yes	–	–
–	R-8 L-3	8am-6:30pm	Yes	–	T
–	R L	8am-10pm	Yes	–	–
V/MC	R-OP L-OP	8am-4pm	Yes	Yes cost varies	E T

Club, **AM**-Amoco, **D**-Discover, **C**-Choice, **R**-restaurant within half mile unless mileage noted, **L**-takeout lunch within half mile unless mileage noted, **OP**-on premises, **E**-public transportation to establishment, **T**-public transportation to Trail, **n/c**-no charge

CAMPGROUNDS, CABINS, AND HOSTELS

Name and Address	Telephone	Miles from Trail	Rates
White Birches Camp Star Rt. 15 Gorham, N.H. 03581	(603) 466-2022 (open 5/30 to 10/12)	1.5	dbl: $10 xp: $2,s,g,c
Cold Spring Camp U.S. 3 Lincoln, N.H. 03251	(603) 745-8351 (seasonal)	4	sgl: $8 dbl: $12 xp: $3
Saco River Camping Area N.H. 16, P.O. Box 546 North Conway, N.H. 03860	(603) 356-3360 (open 5/1 to 10/15)	10	sgl: $12 dbl: $16 g
Pitre's Cabins RFD 1, Box 30, N.H. 112 W North Woodstock, N.H. 03262	(603) 745-8846	5	sgl: $45 dbl: $55 xp: $5
Baker River Campground RFD 1, Box 96, Quincy Rd. Rumney, N.H. 03266	(603) 786-9707	15	sgl: $6-12 dbl: $12 family: $15
Twin Mtn. KOA N.H. 115, P.O. Box 148 Twin Mtn., N.H. 03595	(603) 846-5559 (open 5-10 to 10-15)	6	dbl: $16 xp: $4,c,g, KOA card disc.

Also see **Tamarack Motel and Cabins** under Motels and Hotels.

CODES: sgl-single, **dbl**-double, **g**-group rates, **c**-special rates for children, **s**-senior citizen discount, **xp**-extra person, **MAP**-Modified American Plan, **AP**-American Plan, **B**-breakfast included, **V**-VISA, **MC**-MasterCard, **AE**-American Express, **CB**-Carte Blanche, **DC**-Diners

Credit Cards	Food	Office Open	Park While Hiking	Shuttle to Trail	Public Transportation
–	R-2 L-2	7am- 10pm	Yes	Yes n/c	–
–	R L	24 hrs.	Yes small fee	–	–
V/MC	R L	8am- 9pm	Yes	–	–
–	–	24 hrs.	Yes	–	–
–	R-2.5 L-2.5	9am- 9pm	Yes	–	–
V/MC	R-1.5 L-2.5	8am- 10pm	Yes	–	–

Club, **AM**-Amoco, **D**-Discover, **C**-Choice, **R**-restaurant within half mile unless mileage noted, **L**-takeout lunch within half mile unless mileage noted, **OP**-on premises, **E**-public transportation to establishment, **T**-public transportation to Trail, **n/c**-no charge

Vermont

CONNECTICUT RIVER TO VERMONT-MASSACHUSETTS STATE LINE

Appalachian Trail Guide to New Hampshire and Vermont

Maintaining clubs for this area are the Dartmouth Outing Club and the Green Mountain Club.

GETTING THERE

Air: Scheduled service is available to Rutland State Airport, Hartness State Airport (near Springfield), and Albany, N.Y.
Train: Amtrak stops at White River Junction on a line between Washington, D.C., and Burlington.
Bus: Vermont Transit service directly to the Trail at Sherburne Pass (ask ticket agent about service to "Long Trail Lodge," which is the bus line's term for The Inn at the Long Trail), on a line between Rutland and White River Junction (which has frequent service to many points). Vermont Transit lines cross the Trail at Vt. 103 and Vt. 9. There are no scheduled stops at the crossings, but drivers will usually make a flag stop if notified. The nearest scheduled stop on Vt. 103 is at Cuttingsville, about three miles away, on a line between Rutland and Boston. The nearest on Vt. 9 is at Woodford, about four miles away, on a line between Bennington and Brattleboro. Bennington, just slightly farther away, has frequent service to many points, including several towns just west of the Trail as far north as U.S. 4.
Taxi: Bennington, Brattleboro, Manchester Center, Rutland, West Dover, and White River Junction have taxi companies.

POINTS OF INTEREST

The Long Trail: This 265-mile trail, which predates the Appalachian Trail, runs the length of Vermont from Canada to Massachusetts. A half mile north of U.S. 4, the Appalachian Trail joins the Long Trail, and they coincide for nearly 100 miles to the Vermont-Massachusetts state line.

Killington Peak: The second-highest mountain in Vermont and the highest point on the Appalachian Trail in the state, Killington is about 5.5 miles south of U.S. 4. The climb is steep but rewarding. The actual summit is on a very steep 0.2-mile side trail.
Clarendon Gorge: The Trail crosses the gorge, cut by the Mill River, on a high suspension bridge just a few hundred yards south of Vt. 103.
Lye Brook Wilderness: For about three miles, the Trail passes through this 14,300-acre tract of primitive woodland. The area is equally distant (about six miles) from Vt. 11/30 to the north and the Arlington-West Wardsboro Road to the south. Hiking in either direction is generally on easy to moderate grades.
Stratton Pond: This is the largest body of water on the Long Trail and is very popular for its scenic beauty. It is reached by a moderately steep six-mile hike north from the Arlington-West Wardsboro Road.

ACCESS POINTS

The Trail crosses Vt. 10A, U.S. 5, Vt. 14, Cloudland Road, South Pomfret-Pomfret Road, Barnard Brook Road, Vt. 12, Chatauguay Road (sometimes impassable), River Road, Thundering Brook Road, Vt. 100, U.S. 4, Upper Cold River Road, Lower Cold River Road, Keiffer Lottery Road, Vt. 103, Vt. 140, Danby-Langrove Road (not maintained in winter), Mad Tom Notch Road (not maintained in winter), Vt. 11/30, Arlington-West Wardsboro Road (not maintained in winter), Vt. 9, and County Road (not maintained in winter). The Trail also follows local streets in Norwich and the West Hartford area. Parking is available at all these roads but is very limited in some instances. Most lodgings will allow patrons to park vehicles on their grounds while hiking (see the "Park While Hiking" column in the listings).

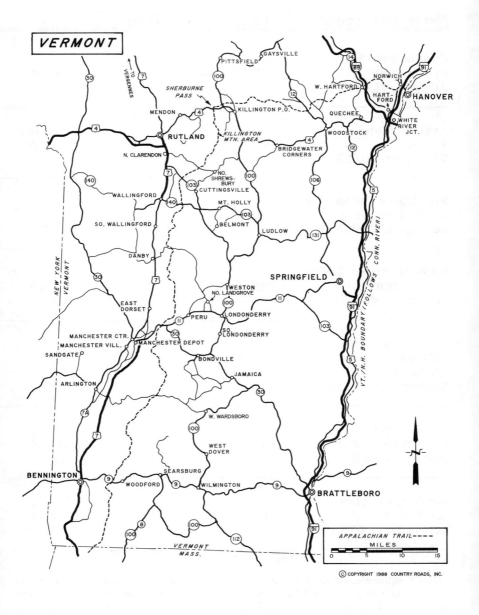

Vermont

MOTELS AND HOTELS

Name and Address	Telephone	Miles from Trail	Rates
Candlelight Motel Rt. 7A North Arlington, Vt. 05250	(802) 375-6647	10	sgl: $37-44 dbl: $48-64
Avalon Motel Vt. 9 East Bennington, Vt. 05201	(802) 442-5485	2	sgl: $31-36 (B) dbl: $35-40 (B) c
Bennington Motor Inn 143 W. Main, Vt. 9 Bennington, Vt. 05201	(802) 442-5479	6	sgl: $34-47 dbl: $36-54 xp: $4
Kirkside Motor Lodge 250 W. Main St. Bennington, Vt. 05201	(802) 447-7596	4	dbl: $34-60 xp: $4
Knotty Pine Motel 130 Northside Drive Historic Rt. 7A Bennington, Vt. 05201	(802) 442-5487	6	sgl: $42-46 dbl: $42-46 xp: $5
Ramada Inn U.S. 7 and Kocher Drive Bennington, Vt. 05201	(802) 442-8145	2	sgl: $59-73 dbl: $67-79 xp: $8,s,c,g
South Gate Motel Box 1073, U.S. 7 Bennington, Vt. 05201	(802) 447-7525	10	sgl: $28-40 dbl: $36-44 xp: $4,c

CODES: sgl-single, **dbl**-double, **g**-group rates, **c**-special rates for children, **s**-senior citizen discount, **xp**-extra person, **MAP**-Modified American Plan, **AP**-American Plan, **B**-breakfast included, **V**-VISA, **MC**-MasterCard, **AE**-American Express, **CB**-Carte Blanche, **DC**-Diners

Credit Cards	Food	Office Open	Park While Hiking	Shuttle to Trail	Public Transportation
V/MC/AE	R L	8am- 11pm	–	–	E
V/MC	R-1 L-1	7am- 10pm	Yes	–	–
V/MC/AE CB/DC	R L	8am- 10:30pm	–	–	–
V/MC/AE	R L	8am- 10pm	Yes	Yes n/c	E
V/MC/AE CB/DC/D	R L	7:30am- 10:30pm	Yes	–	–
V/MC/AE CB/DC/D	R-OP L-OP	24 hrs.	Yes	–	E
V/MC/AE CB/DC/D	R-1.5 L-2	24 hrs.	Yes	–	E

Club, **AM**-Amoco, **D**-Discover, **C**-Choice, **R**-restaurant within half mile unless mileage noted, **L**-takeout lunch within half mile unless mileage noted, **OP**-on premises, **E**-public transportation to establishment, **T**-public transportation to Trail, **n/c**-no charge

MOTELS AND HOTELS

Name and Address	Telephone	Miles from Trail	Rates
The Bradford Motel RFD 1, Box 99, U.S. 7 Danby, Vt. 05739	(802) 293-5186	2	sgl: $35 dbl: $45 g
Marbledge Motor Inn P.O. Box 505, U.S. 7 East Dorset, Vt. 05253	(802) 362-1418	5	sgl: $38-48 dbl: $40-50 xp: $8
Edelweiss Motel & Chalets U.S. 4 Killington, Vt. 05751	(802) 775-5577	1	dbl: $38-99 xp: $5-12,g
Cortina Inn U.S. 4 Killington, Vt. 05751	(800) 451-6108 (802) 773-3331	2	sgl: $40-90 dbl: $60-130 xp: $10-15,s,c,g
Grey Bonnet Inn Vt. 100 N, HCR 65 Killington, Vt. 05751	(802) 775-2537 (closed 4/15 to 6/31 and 10/15 to Thanks.)	.25	dbl: $59 s,c,g
Killington-Pico Motor Inn U.S. 4, HC 34 Killington, Vt. 05751	(802) 773-4088	1	sgl: $34 dbl: $38-48 xp: $5,s,g

CODES: sgl-single, **dbl**-double, **g**-group rates, **c**-special rates for children, **s**-senior citizen discount, **xp**-extra person, **MAP**-Modified American Plan, **AP**-American Plan, **B**-breakfast included, **V**-VISA, **MC**-MasterCard, **AE**-American Express, **CB**-Carte Blanche, **DC**-Diners

Credit Cards	Food	Office Open	Park While Hiking	Shuttle to Trail	Public Transportation
V/MC/AE	R	24 hrs.	Yes	Yes	–
V/MC/AE	R-OP L	7am-10pm	Yes	–	–
V/MC/DC	R	8am-10pm	Yes	–	–
V/MC/AE DC/D	R-OP L-OP	24 hrs.	Yes	Yes n/c	–
V/MC/AE	R	8am-9:30pm	Yes	–	–
V/MC/D	R-OP L	24 hrs.	Yes	–	–

Club, **AM**-Amoco, **D**-Discover, **C**-Choice, **R**-restaurant within half mile unless mileage noted, **L**-takeout lunch within half mile unless mileage noted, **OP**-on premises, **E**-public transportation to establishment, **T**-public transportation to Trail, **n/c**-no charge

MOTELS AND HOTELS

Name and Address	Telephone	Miles from Trail	Rates
North Star Lodge RR 1, Box 3195 Killington Rd. Killington, Vt. 05751	(802) 422-4040 (closed May to mid-June)	4	sgl: $38-130 dbl: $76-220 xp: $10,s,g
Sherburne-Killington Motel HC 34, U.S. 4 Killington, Vt. 05751	(802) 773-9535	1	sgl: $35-48 (B) dbl: $48-56 (B) xp: $8,s,c
Tyrol Motel U.S. 4 Killington, Vt. 05751	(800) 631-1019 (802) 773-7485	3	dbl: $36-98 xp: $5-15
Magic View Motel Vt. 11 Londonderry, Vt. 05148	(802) 824-3793	10	sgl: $28 dbl: $38 xp: $10
Hide Away Motel & Campground RFD 1, Box 725, Rt. 103S Ludlow, Vt. 05149	(802) 228-7871	16	dbl: $45-65 xp: $10,c,g
Inn Towne Motel 112 Main St. Ludlow, Vt. 05149	(802) 228-8884	18	dbl: $39-45 xp: $5

CODES: sgl-single, **dbl**-double, **g**-group rates, **c**-special rates for children, **s**-senior citizen discount, **xp**-extra person, **MAP**-Modified American Plan, **AP**-American Plan, **B**-breakfast included, **V**-VISA, **MC**-MasterCard, **AE**-American Express, **CB**-Carte Blanche, **DC**-Diners

Credit Cards	Food	Office Open	Park While Hiking	Shuttle to Trail	Public Transportation
V/MC/AE	R L	24 hrs.	Yes	–	–
V/MC/AE	R-1 L	7:30am-11pm	Yes	–	E
V/MC	R-OP L-3	7am-11pm	–	–	–
V/MC	R L	9am-10pm	Yes	–	–
V/MC	R L	–	Yes	–	E T
V/MC/AE	R L	7am-midnight	Yes	–	–

Club, AM-Amoco, D-Discover, C-Choice, R-restaurant within half mile unless mileage noted, L-takeout lunch within half mile unless mileage noted, OP-on premises, E-public transportation to establishment, T-public transportation to Trail, n/c-no charge

MOTELS AND HOTELS

Name and Address	Telephone	Miles from Trail	Rates
Okemo Mtn. Ski Area Lodging Office RFD 1 Ludlow, Vt. 05149	(802) 228-5571	8	dbl: $75 and up g
Sunderland Motel P.O. Box 375 Manchester, Vt. 05254	(802) 362-1176 (closed part of Nov. and April)	5	sgl: $40-50 dbl: $50-60 xp: $8
Mendon Mountain Orchards Motel Rt. 4 Mendon, Vt. 05701	(802) 775-5477	2.5	sgl: $24-45 dbl: $26-45 xp: $3
Country Squire Motel U.S. 7B & Vt. 103 Box 224 North Clarendon, Vt. 05759	(802) 773-3805	2	sgl: $30 (B) dbl: $40-45 (B) xp: $5,s
Bromley Sun Lodge Rt. 11 Peru, Vt. 05152	(802) 824-6941	1	sgl: $35-85 dbl: $45-95 xp: $6-15,s,c,g
Comfort Inn 170 S. Main St. Rutland, Vt. 05701	(802) 775-2200	10	sgl: $48-120 dbl: $58-120 xp: $5,s,c,g

CODES: sgl-single, **dbl**-double, **g**-group rates, **c**-special rates for children, **s**-senior citizen discount, **xp**-extra person, **MAP**-Modified American Plan, **AP**-American Plan, **B**-breakfast included, **V**-VISA, **MC**-MasterCard, **AE**-American Express, **CB**-Carte Blanche, **DC**-Diners

Credit Cards	Food	Office Open	Park While Hiking	Shuttle to Trail	Public Transportation
V/MC/AE	R-OP L-1	8am-4:30pm	Yes	–	–
V/MC/AE	R-1 L-OP	7:30am-10pm	–	–	–
V/MC	R L-OP	8am-12pm	Yes	Yes n/c	E
V/MC/AE	R-4 L-1	8am-11pm	Yes	–	–
V/MC/AE D	R-OP L-OP	7am-midnight	Yes	Yes n/c	–
V/MC/AE CB/DC/D	R-OP L-OP	24 hrs.	Yes	–	E

Club, **AM**-Amoco, **D**-Discover, **C**-Choice, **R**-restaurant within half mile unless mileage noted, **L**-takeout lunch within half mile unless mileage noted, **OP**-on premises, **E**-public transportation to establishment, **T**-public transportation to Trail, **n/c**-no charge

MOTELS AND HOTELS

Name and Address	Telephone	Miles from Trail	Rates
Rutland Motel 125 Woodstock Ave. Rutland, Vt. 05701	(802) 775-4348	10	sgl: $32-45 dbl: $34-53 xp: $3
Motel on the Mountain Vt. 9, HCR 65, Box 22 Searsburg, Vt. 05363	(802) 464-8233	9	sgl: $30-50 dbl: $35-55 xp: $5-15
Hotel Coolidge 17 South Main P.O. Box 515 White River Jct., Vt. 05001	(800) 622-1124 (802) 295-3118	5	sgl: $22-57 dbl: $28-89 xp: $5,s,c,g
Maple Leaf Motel & Campground U.S. 5, RR1, Box 54 White River Jct., Vt. 05001	(802) 295-2817	8	sgl: $30-40 dbl: $38-48 xp: $5
Susse Chalet Motor Lodge Vt. 5 White River Jct. Vt. 05001	(802) 295-3051	5	sgl: $33-37 dbl: $40-50 xp: $3-5
Crafts Inn West Main St. Wilmington, Vt. 05363	(802) 464-2344	15	dbl: $120 xp: $20

CODES: sgl-single, **dbl**-double, **g**-group rates, **c**-special rates for children, **s**-senior citizen discount, **xp**-extra person, **MAP**-Modified American Plan, **AP**-American Plan, **B**-breakfast included, **V**-VISA, **MC**-MasterCard, **AE**-American Express, **CB**-Carte Blanche, **DC**-Diners

Credit Cards	Food	Office Open	Park While Hiking	Shuttle to Trail	Public Transportation
V/MC/AE	R	7am-11pm	–	–	–
V/MC/D	R-6 L-8	8am-11pm	Yes	–	–
V/MC/AE D	R L	24 hrs.	Yes	–	E T
V/MC	R-2 L-2	7:30am-11pm	Yes	–	–
V/MC/AE	R L	24 hrs.	Yes	–	–
V/MC/AE	R-OP L	–	Yes	–	–

Club, **AM**-Amoco, **D**-Discover, **C**-Choice, **R**-restaurant within half mile unless mileage noted, **L**-takeout lunch within half mile unless mileage noted, **OP**-on premises, **E**-public transportation to establishment, **T**-public transportation to Trail, **n/c**-no charge

MOTELS AND HOTELS

Name and Address	Telephone	Miles from Trail	Rates
Vintage Motel W. Main St. Vt. 9, P.O. Box 222 Wilmington, Vt. 05363	(802) 464-8824	14	sgl: $35 (B) dbl: $48 (B) xp: $5
Braeside Motel P.O. Box 411, U.S. 4 Woodstock, Vt. 05091	(802) 457-1366	22	sgl: $42-74 (B) dbl: $46-78 (B) xp: $8,c

BED AND BREAKFASTS AND COUNTRY

The Arlington Inn Historic Rt. 7A Arlington, Vt. 05250	(802) 375-6532	5	sgl: $50-125 dbl: $50-125 xp: $12,g
The Inn on Covered Bridge Green RD 1, Box 3550 Arlington, Vt. 05250	(802) 375-9489	15	sgl: $45 (B) dbl: $90 (B) xp: $20
Ira Allen House RD 2, Box 2485, Rt. 7A Arlington, Vt. 05250	(802) 362-2284 (open May to March)	5	sgl: $30-40 dbl: $50-60 xp: $20,g
Shenandoah Farm Arlington, Vt. 05250	(802) 375-6372	12	sgl: $35-40 (B) dbl: $60-70 (B)

CODES: sgl-single, **dbl**-double, **g**-group rates, **c**-special rates for children, **s**-senior citizen discount, **xp**-extra person, **MAP**-Modified American Plan, **AP**-American Plan, **B**-breakfast included, **V**-VISA, **MC**-MasterCard, **AE**-American Express, **CB**-Carte Blanche, **DC**-Diners

Credit Cards	Food	Office Open	Park While Hiking	Shuttle to Trail	Public Transportation
V/MC/AE	R L-.75	24 hrs.	Yes	–	–
V/MC/AE	R L-OP	7:30am-10pm	Yes	–	–

INNS

Credit Cards	Food	Office Open	Park While Hiking	Shuttle to Trail	Public Transportation
V/MC/AE	R-OP L	24 hrs.	Yes	–	E
–	R-OP L	6:30am-10pm	Yes	–	–
V/MC/AE	R-2 L-3	7am-11pm	Yes	–	–
–	R-5 L-7	24 hrs.	Yes	–	–

Club, **AM**-Amoco, **D**-Discover, **C**-Choice, **R**-restaurant within half mile unless mileage noted, **L**-takeout lunch within half mile unless mileage noted, **OP**-on premises, **E**-public transportation to establishment, **T**-public transportation to Trail, **n/c**-no charge

BED AND BREAKFASTS AND COUNTRY

Name and Address	Telephone	Miles from Trail	Rates
The Parmenter House Church St., P.O. Box 106 Belmont, Vt. 05730	(802) 259-2009	7	sgl: $50 (B) dbl: $60-85 (B) xp: $15
Molly Stark Inn 1067 East Main St. Bennington, Vt. 05201	(802) 442-9631	3	sgl: $47 (B) dbl: $57 (B) xp: $10,s,g
Alpenrose Inn Winhall Hollow Rd. Bondville, Vt. 05340	(802) 297-2750 (closed April to June 15 and November)	3	sgl: $60 dbl: $75 xp: $30,g
Bromley View Inn Vt. 30, RR1, Box 161 Bondville, Vt. 05340-9705	(802) 297-1459	2	sgl: $30-44 (B) dbl: $60-88 (B) xp: $15-25,s,c,g
October Country Inn Box 66, Upper Rd. U.S. 4 & Vt. 100A Bridgewater Corners, Vt. 05035	(802) 672-3412 (open 11/20 to 3/31 and 5/1 to 10/31)	8	sgl: $65-80 (MAP) dbl: $100-130 (MAP) xp: $45,c,g
Quails Nest B&B Inn Main St., P.O. Box 221 Danby, Vt. 05739	(802) 293-5099	3	sgl: $35-45 (B) dbl: $45-55 (B) xp: $15
Silas Griffith Inn South Main St. RR 1, Box 66F Danby, Vt. 05739	(802) 293-5567	2	sgl: $55-65 (B) dbl: $65-78 (B) xp: $10,c,g

CODES: **sgl**-single, **dbl**-double, **g**-group rates, **c**-special rates for children, **s**-senior citizen discount, **xp**-extra person, **MAP**-Modified American Plan, **AP**-American Plan, **B**-breakfast included, **V**-VISA, **MC**-MasterCard, **AE**-American Express, **CB**-Carte Blanche, **DC**-Diners

INNS

Credit Cards	Food	Office Open	Park While Hiking	Shuttle to Trail	Public Transportation
V/MC	R-4 L	8am-10pm	Yes	Yes n/c	–
V/MC	R L-OP	24 hrs.	Yes	Yes n/c	–
–	R	24 hrs.	Yes	–	–
V/MC/AE	R-OP L-4	8am-10pm	Yes	Yes n/c	–
V/MC	R-OP L	24 hrs.	Yes	Yes	E
V/MC	R L	8am-10pm	Yes	–	E
V/MC/AE	R-OP L	8am-10pm	Yes	Yes n/c	–

Club, **AM**-Amoco, **D**-Discover, **C**-Choice, **R**-restaurant within half mile unless mileage noted, **L**-takeout lunch within half mile unless mileage noted, **OP**-on premises, **E**-public transportation to establishment, **T**-public transportation to Trail, **n/c**-no charge

BED AND BREAKFASTS AND COUNTRY

Name and Address	Telephone	Miles from Trail	Rates
Christmas Tree B&B RR 1, Box 382 Benedict Rd. East Dorset, Vt. 05253	(802) 362-4889	6	sgl: $25-30 (B) dbl: $45-55 (B) xp: $10
House of Seven Gables 221 Main St., Box 526 Hartford, Vt. 05047	(802) 295-1200	5	sgl: $35-45 (B) dbl: $50-65 (B) xp: $10,c,g
Three Mountain Inn Box 180, Vt. 30 Jamaica, Vt. 05343	(802) 874-4140 (open June to mid-Nov., mid-Dec. to April)	15	dbl: $65-85 (MAP) xp: $45,g
The Inn at the Long Trail Sherburne Pass, U.S. 4 P.O. Box 267 Killington, Vt. 05751	(800) 325-3540 (802) 775-7181 (open 7/1 to 10/24 and 11/26 to 4/14)	on Trail	dbl: $24-34 (B) (MAP in fall) xp: $16-26,s
Mountain Meadows Lodge Thundering Brook Rd. RR 1, Box 2080 Killington, Vt. 05751	(802) 775-1010 (open June to mid-Oct. and Thanks. to mid-April)	on Trail	sgl: $55 (MAP) dbl: $90 (MAP) xp: $22,c,g
Trailside Lodge HCR 65, Coffee House Rd. Killington, Vt. 05751	(802) 422-3532 (800) 447-2209	2	sgl: $35-45 dbl: $35-45 xp: $8,c,g

CODES: sgl-single, **dbl**-double, **g**-group rates, **c**-special rates for children, **s**-senior citizen discount, **xp**-extra person, **MAP**-Modified American Plan, **AP**-American Plan, **B**-breakfast included, **V**-VISA, **MC**-MasterCard, **AE**-American Express, **CB**-Carte Blanche, **DC**-Diners

INNS

Credit Cards	Food	Office Open	Park While Hiking	Shuttle to Trail	Public Transportation
–	R-1 L-1	8am-10:30pm	Yes	Yes n/c	–
V/MC/AE	R L-OP	24 hrs.	Yes	–	–
–	R-OP L	8am-10pm	Yes	–	–
V/MC	R-OP L-1	8am-11pm	Yes	–	E
V/MC	R-OP L-OP	8am-8pm	Yes	Yes $10	–
V/MC	R L-2.5	7am-midnight	Yes	–	E

Club, **AM**-Amoco, **D**-Discover, **C**-Choice, **R**-restaurant within half mile unless mileage noted, **L**-takeout lunch within half mile unless mileage noted, **OP**-on premises, **E**-public transportation to establishment, **T**-public transportation to Trail, **n/c**-no charge

BED AND BREAKFASTS AND COUNTRY

Name and Address	Telephone	Miles from Trail	Rates
The Vermont Inn Rt. 4 Killington, Vt. 05751	(800) 541-7795 (802) 775-0708 (open 6/1 to 10/23 11/20 to 3/31)	2	dbl: $50-80 (MAP) xp: $40-45 (MAP)
The Country Hare HCR Box 1A Vt. 11 & Magic Mtn. Rd. Londonderry, Vt. 05148	(802) 824-3131 (closed one week in April and Nov.)	10	sgl: $35-70 (B) dbl: $45-90 (B) xp: $15-20,g
Greenmount Lodge P.O. Box 312 Londonderry, Vt. 05148	(802) 824-5948	7	sgl: $30-40 dbl: $45-60 g
Inn on Magic Mtn. RFD 1, Box 30 Magic Mtn. Access Rd. Londonderry, Vt. 05148	(802) 824-6100	8	sgl: $48 dbl: $98 s,c,g
Black River Inn 100 Main St. Ludlow, Vt. 05149	(802) 228-5585	10	sgl: $78 (MAP) dbl: $135 (MAP) g
The Combes Family Inn RFD 1, Box 275 Ludlow, Vt. 05149	(802) 228-8799	16	sgl: $66-76 dbl: $76-86 xp: $10-15,g

CODES: **sgl**-single, **dbl**-double, **g**-group rates, **c**-special rates for children, **s**-senior citizen discount, **xp**-extra person, **MAP**-Modified American Plan, **AP**-American Plan, **B**-breakfast included, **V**-VISA, **MC**-MasterCard, **AE**-American Express, **CB**-Carte Blanche, **DC**-Diners

INNS

Credit Cards	Food	Office Open	Park While Hiking	Shuttle to Trail	Public Transportation
V/MC/AE	R-OP L-1	8am-11pm	Yes	–	–
V/MC/D	R L-1	7am-11pm	Yes	Yes	–
V/MC/AE	R-OP L-OP	8am-9pm	Yes	–	–
V/MC/DC	R-OP L-OP	8am-10pm	Yes	–	–
V/MC/AE	R-OP L-OP	8am-10pm	Yes	–	E
V/MC/AE	R-OP L-OP	24 hrs.	Yes	Yes n/c	E

Club, **AM**-Amoco, **D**-Discover, **C**-Choice, **R**-restaurant within half mile unless mileage noted, **L**-takeout lunch within half mile unless mileage noted, **OP**-on premises, **E**-public transportation to establishment, **T**-public transportation to Trail, **n/c**-no charge

BED AND BREAKFASTS AND COUNTRY

Name and Address	Telephone	Miles from Trail	Rates
Jewell Brook Inn 82 Andover St., Vt. 100 Ludlow, Vt. 05149	(802) 228-8926 (closed two weeks in Nov. and May)	16	sgl: $55 (B) dbl: $75 (B) xp: $13
Brook-n-Hearth Vt. 11/30, P.O. Box 508 Manchester Ctr., Vt. 05255	(802) 362-3604 (open 5/25 to 10/31, 11/25 to 4/21)	3	sgl: $36-40 (B) dbl: $50-60 (B) xp: $15-20,c
The Inn At Manchester Rt. 7A, Box 41 Manchester, Vt. 05254	(802) 362-1793	5	dbl: $55-90 (B) xp: $15
Wilburton Inn River Rd. Manchester, Vt. 05254	(802) 362-1788	6	sgl: $30-45 (B) g
Red Clover Inn Woodward Rd. Mendon, Vt. 05701	(802) 775-2290 (closed two weeks in April)	3	sgl: $104-114 (MAP) dbl: $130-145 (MAP) xp: $35
The Hortonville Inn Hortonville Rd. Mount Holly, Vt. 05758	(802) 259-2587	5	sgl: $35 dbl: $40 xp: $10
Johnny Seesaw's P.O. Box 68, Vt. 11 Peru, Vt. 05152	(802) 824-5533 (open mid-May to late Oct., Thanks. to mid-Apr.)	2	rates vary (B, summer & fall, MAP, winter) c,g

CODES: **sgl**-single, **dbl**-double, **g**-group rates, **c**-special rates for children, **s**-senior citizen discount, **xp**-extra person, **MAP**-Modified American Plan, **AP**-American Plan, **B**-breakfast included, **V**-VISA, **MC**-MasterCard, **AE**-American Express, **CB**-Carte Blanche, **DC**-Diners

INNS

Credit Cards	Food	Office Open	Park While Hiking	Shuttle to Trail	Public Transportation
V/MC/AE	R	9am-10pm	Yes	Yes	–
V/MC/AE	R L	7am-11pm	Yes	Yes $.50/mile	–
V/MC/AE	R L	8am-11pm	Yes	Yes	E
V/MC/AE	R-OP L-OP	9am-9pm	Yes	Yes	–
V/MC/AE DC	R-OP L-OP	8am-9pm	Yes	Yes n/c	–
V/MC	R-1.5 L	8am-11pm	Yes	Yes	–
V/MC/AE	R-OP L	8am-10pm	Yes	Yes	–

Club, **AM**-Amoco, **D**-Discover, **C**-Choice, **R**-restaurant within half mile unless mileage noted, **L**-takeout lunch within half mile unless mileage noted, **OP**-on premises, **E**-public transportation to establishment, **T**-public transportation to Trail, **n/c**-no charge

Vermont

BED AND BREAKFASTS AND COUNTRY

Name and Address	Telephone	Miles from Trail	Rates
Pittsfield Inn Vt. 100, P.O. Box 526 Pittsfield, Vt. 05762	(802) 746-8943	7	sgl: $49-69 dbl: $49-69 xp: $20
Swiss Farm Lodge Vt. 100 N, P.O. Box 517 Pittsfield, Vt. 05762	(802) 746-8341	10	sgl: $20 (B) dbl: $40 (B) xp: $10,c
The Inn at Rutland 70 N. Main St. Rutland, Vt. 05701	(802) 773-0575	6	sgl: $60-75 (B) dbl: $80-95 (B) xp: $20
The Evergreen Inn Sandgate Rd., Box 2480 Sandgate, Vt. 05250	(802) 375-2272 (open 5/15 to 10/15)	20	sgl: $22-26 (B) dbl: $42-50 (B) c
The Londonderry Inn Vt. 100, P.O. Box 301 South Londonderry, Vt. 05155	(802) 824-5226	13	sgl: $24-69 (B) dbl: $29-69 (B) xp: $9-18,c
The Green Mountain Tea Room RR 1, Box 400, Vt. 7 South Wallingford, Vt. 05773	(802) 446-2611	2.5	sgl: $40 dbl: $50
Strong House Inn RD 1, Box 9 Vergennes, Vt. 05491	(802) 877-3337	40	sgl: $35-55 (B) dbl: $45-70 (B) xp: $10

CODES: sgl-single, **dbl**-double, **g**-group rates, **c**-special rates for children, **s**-senior citizen discount, **xp**-extra person, **MAP**-Modified American Plan, **AP**-American Plan, **B**-breakfast included, **V**-VISA, **MC**-MasterCard, **AE**-American Express, **CB**-Carte Blanche, **DC**-Diners

INNS

Credit Cards	Food	Office Open	Park While Hiking	Shuttle to Trail	Public Trans- portation
V/MC	R-OP L	8am-9pm	Yes	Yes n/c	E
–	R-1.5 L	7am-10pm	Yes	–	–
V/MC	R L	24 hrs.	Yes	Yes	–
–	R-OP L-OP	24 hrs.	Yes	–	–
–	R-OP L-1	7am-11pm	Yes	–	–
V/MC	R-OP L-OP	24 hrs.	Yes	Yes	E
V/MC	R L	8am-9pm	Yes	–	E

Club, **AM**-Amoco, **D**-Discover, **C**-Choice, **R**-restaurant within half mile unless mileage noted, **L**-takeout lunch within half mile unless mileage noted, **OP**-on premises, **E**-public transportation to establishment, **T**-public transportation to Trail, **n/c**-no charge

BED AND BREAKFASTS AND COUNTRY

Name and Address	Telephone	Miles from Trail	Rates
Dunham House 7 S. Main St., Box 338 Wallingford, Vt. 05773	(802) 446-2600	4	sgl: $25-45 (B) dbl: $45-65 (B) xp: $10-15,g
White Rocks Inn RR 1, Box 297 Wallingford, Vt. 05773	(802) 446-2077 (closed Nov.)	2	dbl: $60-85 xp: $15
The Gray Ghost Inn Vt. 100, P.O. Box 938 West Dover, Vt. 05356	(802) 464-2474	12	sgl: $30 (B) dbl: $50 (B) c,g
Kitzhof Lodge Vt. 100, HCR 63, Box 14 West Dover, Vt. 05356	(802) 464-8310 (closed April and 10/20 to11/15)	5	sgl: $48 (B) dbl: $58 (B) xp:$22,s,g,c
Weathervane Lodge Box 51, Dorr Fitch Rd. West Dover, Vt. 05356	(802) 464-5426	10	sgl: $28-40 (B) dbl: $36-60 (B) c
West Dover Inn P.O. Box 506, Vt. 100 West Dover, Vt. 05356	(802) 464-5207 (closed Easter to 7/1, 1 week in late fall)	12	dbl: $65-135 (B) xp: $15-25,g
Colonial House Inn Vt. 100, Box 138 Weston, Vt. 05161	(802) 824-6286	8	sgl: $35-46 dbl: $56-78 xp: $16,s,c

CODES: sgl-single, **dbl**-double, **g**-group rates, **c**-special rates for children, **s**-senior citizen discount, **xp**-extra person, **MAP**-Modified American Plan, **AP**-American Plan, **B**-breakfast included, **V**-VISA, **MC**-MasterCard, **AE**-American Express, **CB**-Carte Blanche, **DC**-Diners

INNS

Credit Cards	Food	Office Open	Park While Hiking	Shuttle to Trail	Public Transportation
V/MC	R L	24 hrs.	Yes	Yes n/c	E
V/MC	R-1.5 L-1.5	8am-10pm	Yes	Yes	–
V/MC/AE D	R L	7am-10pm	Yes	–	–
V/MC	R-OP L-1.25	6am-11pm	Yes	Yes $20	–
–	R-1 L-1	24 hrs.	Yes	–	–
V/AE	R-OP L	7:30am-11pm	Yes	–	–
V/MC	R-OP L-2	8am-10pm	Yes	–	–

Club, **AM**-Amoco, **D**-Discover, **C**-Choice, **R**-restaurant within half mile unless mileage noted, **L**-takeout lunch within half mile unless mileage noted, **OP**-on premises, **E**-public transportation to establishment, **T**-public transportation to Trail, **n/c**-no charge

BED AND BREAKFASTS AND COUNTRY

Name and Address	Telephone	Miles from Trail	Rates
Fjord Gate Inn & Farm RR 1, Box 138F Higley Hill Rd. Wilmington, Vt. 05363	(802) 464-2783	20	sgl: $20 dbl: $36-85 xp: $5-24,c,g
Nordic Hills Lodge 179 Coldbrook Rd. Wilmington, Vt. 05363	(802) 464-5130	10	sgl: $40-50 dbl: $46-56 xp: $8,c,g
Carriage House of Woodstock Vt. 4 W Woodstock, Vt. 05091	(802) 457-4322	4	sgl: $75-85 (B) xp: $15,g
Three Church Street Inn 3 Church St. Woodstock, Vt. 05091	(802) 457-1925 (closed April)	3	dbl: $62-78 xp: $20
Woodstock House Vt. 106, P.O. Box 361 Woodstock, Vt. 05091	(802) 457-1758	5	sgl: $30-40 dbl: $50-70 xp: $15

CAMPGROUNDS, CABINS, AND HOSTELS

Name and Address	Telephone	Miles from Trail	Rates
Otter Creek Campground U.S. 7 Danby, Vt. 05739	(802) 293-5041	4	dbl: $9/site xp: $2,g

CODES: sgl-single, **dbl**-double, **g**-group rates, **c**-special rates for children, **s**-senior citizen discount, **xp**-extra person, **MAP**-Modified American Plan, **AP**-American Plan, **B**-breakfast included, **V**-VISA, **MC**-MasterCard, **AE**-American Express, **CB**-Carte Blanche, **DC**-Diners

INNS

Credit Cards	Food	Office Open	Park While Hiking	Shuttle to Trail	Public Transportation
V/MC	R-OP L-OP	24 hrs.	Yes	Yes $7	–
V/MC/AE DC	R-1.5 L-1.5	8am- 11pm	Yes	–	–
V/MC	R-1 L	9am- 9pm	Yes	–	–
V/MC	R L	7am- 7pm	Yes	–	–
V	R-1 L-OP	7:30am- 8:30pm	Yes	–	–
–	R-2 L-2	8am- 9pm	Yes	–	–

Club, **AM**-Amoco, **D**-Discover, **C**-Choice, **R**-restaurant within half mile unless mileage noted, **L**-takeout lunch within half mile unless mileage noted, **OP**-on premises, **E**-public transportation to establishment, **T**-public transportation to Trail, **n/c**-no charge

CAMPGROUNDS, CABINS, AND HOSTELS

Name and Address	Telephone	Miles from Trail	Rates
White River Valley Camping Vt. 107 Gaysville, Vt. 05746	(802) 234-9115 (open Dec.to Feb., April to Oct.)	20	$12-16/site xp: $3,c
Greenwood Lodge & Tentsites (P.O. Box 246 Bennington, Vt. 05201) Vt. 9 Woodford, Vt. 05201	(802) 442-2547 (914) 472-2575	3	sgl: $14 xp: $10,c AYH mbr. disc.

Also see **Maple Leaf Motel and Campground** and **Hide Away Motel**

CODES: sgl-single, **dbl**-double, **g**-group rates, **c**-special rates for children, **s**-senior citizen discount, **xp**-extra person, **MAP**-Modified American Plan, **AP**-American Plan, **B**-breakfast included, **V**-VISA, **MC**-MasterCard, **AE**-American Express, **CB**-Carte Blanche, **DC**-Diners

Credit Cards	Food	Office Open	Park While Hiking	Shuttle to Trail	Public Transportation
V/MC	R L	9am-8pm	Yes	–	–
–	R-8 L-8	7am-10pm	Yes	–	E

and Campground under Motels and Hotels

Club, **AM**-Amoco, **D**-Discover, **C**-Choice, **R**-restaurant within half mile unless mileage noted, **L**-takeout lunch within half mile unless mileage noted, **OP**-on premises, **E**-public transportation to establishment, **T**-public transportation to Trail, **n/c**-no charge

MASSACHUSETTS

VERMONT-MASSACHUSETTS STATE LINE TO MASSACHUSETTS-CONNECTICUT STATE LINE

Appalachian Trail Guide to Massachusetts-Connecticut

The maintaining club for this area is the Berkshire Chapter of the Appalachian Mountain Club.

GETTING THERE

Air: The nearest airports with scheduled service are in Albany, N.Y., and Hartford, Conn.
Train: Amtrak stops at Pittsfield on a line between Albany and Boston.
Bus: Berkshire Regional Transit Authority, (413) 499-2782, provides local service directly to the Trail at South and Main streets in Dalton. The service runs Monday through Saturday between Pittsfield and Hinsdale. Englander Coach Lines provides service to North Adams, which is on the Trail, on a line linking Boston with Williamstown and Bennington, Vt. The Bonanza bus line also has a daily run between North Adams and New York City. Bonanza has several runs a day between New York City, Pittsfield, and Bennington that cross the Trail at U.S. 7; however, there is no scheduled stop at the Trail crossing. The nearest stops are in Great Barrington and Sheffield, both about four miles away in opposite directions. Several lines cross the Trail on the Massachusetts Turnpike. They are a Greyhound line between Boston and Buffalo, N.Y., and Cleveland, Ohio; a Peter Pan line between Albany and Boston; a Bonanza line between Providence, R.I., and Albany; and an Arrow Line line between Bridgeport, Conn., and Albany (very limited service). The nearest stop is in Lee, about five miles away from the Trail.
Taxi: Great Barrington, Lee, Pittsfield, and Stockbridge have taxi companies.

POINTS OF INTEREST

Mt. Greylock: At the summit of the highest peak in Massachusetts (3,491 feet) are the Massachusetts War Memorial Tower and Bascom Lodge, operated by the Appalachian Mountain Club and the state of Massachusetts. A resident naturalist and staff members provide programs for visitors in the summer. A seasonal auto road leads to the summit. From there, the Trail leads north about six miles to North Adams (crossing summit approach road twice), with several steep sections, and south about eight miles to Cheshire (also crossing summit approach road twice), with somewhat less steep grades.

Upper Goose Pond: This pristine body of water is the centerpiece of a protected natural area that includes historical remains and a camping area. It is reached by a moderately difficult hike about two miles south of U.S. 20.

Jug End: There are spectacular views from the point where the Taconic Range juts out over a valley. The climb south from Jug End Road is only a mile long but steep.

Mt. Everett: There are magnificent views in all directions from the open 2,602-foot summit (ninth highest in the state), known as the Dome of the Taconics. It is reached by a moderately difficult trail about a mile south from the Guilder Pond Picnic Area.

Race Mountain: The summit (2,365 feet) is about two miles south of Mt. Everett. The Trail in this area follows close to an open cliff with views.

ACCESS POINTS

Parking is available at most road crossings but is very limited at some. Sometimes the best location is a short distance away, rather than at the crossing itself. The Trail follows several local streets in North Adams (check at Greylock Community Club, 100 yards east of the Trail on Mass. 2, about parking), Cheshire, Dalton, and Tyringham. It also crosses Notch Road, Summit Road (large parking lot at summit of Mt. Greylock), Rockwell Road, Pittsfield Road, County Road (dirt), Tyne (Becket) Road, U.S. 20 (park 0.3 mile west of crossing), Goose Pond (Tyringham) Road (dirt; Trail follows it a short distance), Blue Hill Road, Mass. 23 (Trail follows it about a half mile), Lake Buel Road, Homes Road, Kellogg Road (Trail follows it about a half mile), U.S. 7 (Trail follows it a short distance), Lime Kiln Road and South Egremont Road (which, together, the Trail follows about two miles), Mass. 41, Jug End Road (small parking area), and roads in Guilder Pond Picnic area. Most lodgings will allow patrons to park vehicles on their grounds while hiking (see the "Park While Hiking" column in the listings).

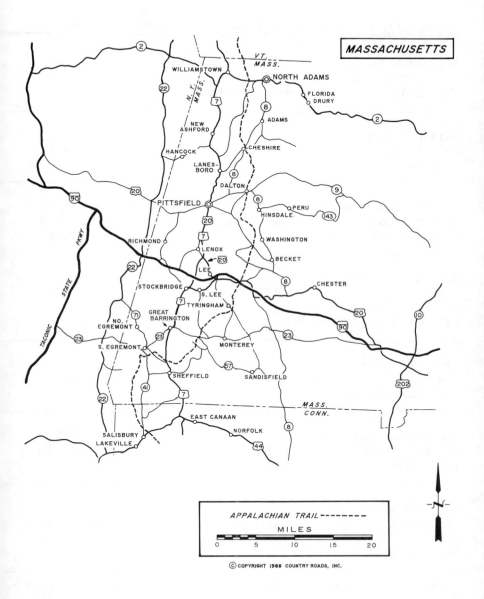

MOTELS AND HOTELS

Name and Address	Telephone	Miles from Trail	Rates
Whitcomb Summit Motel (North Adams, Mass. 01247) Florida, Mass.	(413) 662-2625 (open 5/30 to 10/31)	12	sgl: $40 dbl: $45 xp: $5
Berkshire Motor Inn 372 Main St. Great Barrington, Mass. 01230	(413) 528-3150	2	sgl: $45 dbl: $85 xp: $5,s,g
Lantern House Motel Stockbridge Rd., U.S. 7 Great Barrington, Mass. 01230	(413) 528-2350	0.5	sgl: $38-75 dbl: $40-80 xp: $5,g
Monument Mountain Motel U.S. 7, 249 Stockbridge Rd. Great Barrington, Mass. 01230	(413) 528-3272	3	sgl: $35 dbl: $90 xp: $5-10
Mountain View Motel 304 State Rd., Mass. 23 East Great Barrington, Mass. 01230	(413) 528-0250	2.5	$35-95
Tanglewood Motor Inn P.O. Box 116, U.S. 7 & 20 Lenox, Mass. 01240	(413) 442-4000	15	sgl: $32-98 dbl: $38-105 s,g
Best Western Springs Motor Inn U.S. 7 New Ashford, Mass. 01237	(413) 458-5945	6.5	sgl: $40-85 dbl: $60-99 xp: $9, s,c,g

CODES: sgl-single, **dbl**-double, **g**-group rates, **c**-special rates for children, **s**-senior citizen discount, **xp**-extra person, **MAP**-Modified American Plan, **AP**-American Plan, **B**-breakfast included, **V**-VISA, **MC**-MasterCard, **AE**-American Express, **CB**-Carte Blanche, **DC**-Diners

Credit Cards	Food	Office Open	Park While Hiking	Shuttle to Trail	Public Transportation
V/MC/AE DC	R-OP L-OP	24 hrs.	Yes	–	–
V/MC/AE	R	24 hrs.	Yes	–	–
V/MC	R L	8am-2pm	Yes	–	E
V/MC/AE DC/D	R L	8am-11pm	limited	–	E
V/MC/AE	R L	8am-11pm	Yes	Yes n/c	–
V/MC/AE	R L	24 hrs.	Yes	–	E T
V/MC/AE CB/DC/AM/D	R-OP L-OP	24 hrs.	Yes	–	–

Club, **AM**-Amoco, **D**-Discover, **C**-Choice, **R**-restaurant within half mile unless mileage noted, **L**-takeout lunch within half mile unless mileage noted, **OP**-on premises, **E**-public transportation to establishment, **T**-public transportation to Trail, **n/c**-no charge

Massachusetts

MOTELS AND HOTELS

Name and Address	Telephone	Miles from Trail	Rates
Brodie Mountain Ski Resort U.S. 7 New Ashford, Mass. 01237	(413) 443-4752	7	sgl: $35-55 dbl: $60-130 xp: $5
Carriage House Motel U.S. 7 New Ashford, Mass. 01237	(413) 458-5359	5.5	sgl: $45-48 dbl: $45-55 xp: $5,s,c,g
Days Inn 40 Main St. North Adams, Mass. 01247	(413) 664-4561	5	sgl: $55 dbl: $65 xp: $10,g
Pittsfield Travelodge 16 Cheshire Rd. Pittsfield, Mass. 01201	(413) 443-5661	2	sgl: $52 dbl: $61 xp: $6,s,g
The Depot Guest House Mass. 7A Sheffield, Mass. 01257	(413) 229-8894	2	sgl: $38-55 dbl: $40-55
Stagecoach Hill Inn Mass. 41, Undermountain Rd. Sheffield, Mass. 01257	(413) 229-8585	0.5	sgl: $35-45 dbl: $55-65 xp: $15,c,g
Cozy Corner Motel U.S. 7 & Sand Springs Rd. Williamstown, Mass. 01267	(413) 458-8006	5	sgl: $43-63 db: $45-65 xp: $5, g

CODES: sgl-single, **dbl**-double, **g**-group rates, **c**-special rates for children, **s**-senior citizen discount, **xp**-extra person, **MAP**-Modified American Plan, **AP**-American Plan, **B**-breakfast included, **V**-VISA, **MC**-MasterCard, **AE**-American Express, **CB**-Carte Blanche, **DC**-Diners

Credit Cards	Food	Office Open	Park While Hiking	Shuttle to Trail	Public Transportation
V/MC/AE D	R L-1	9am-4:30pm	Yes	–	–
V/MC/AE	R	9am-11pm	Yes	–	–
V/MC/AE DC	R-OP L-OP	24 hrs.	Yes	–	E
all major	R-OP L-OP	6am-10pm	Yes	–	–
V/MC	R L	24 hrs.	Yes	Yes n/c	–
V/MC/AE DC	R-OP L-7	8am-11pm	Yes	–	–
V/MC/AE	R-OP L	24 hrs.	Yes	–	–

Club, **AM**-Amoco, **D**-Discover, **C**-Choice, **R**-restaurant within half mile unless mileage noted, **L**-takeout lunch within half mile unless mileage noted, **OP**-on premises, **E**-public transportation to establishment, **T**-public transportation to Trail, **n/c**-no charge

MOTELS AND HOTELS

Name and Address	Telephone	Miles from Trail	Rates
The 1896 Motel U.S. 7 and Mass. 2 Williamstown, Mass. 01267	(413) 458-8125	3	sgl: $40-67 (B) dbl: $45-72 (B) xp: $7, s,c,g
Elwal Pines Motor Inn 811 Cold Spring Rd. U.S. 7 & Mass. 2 Williamstown, Mass. 01267	(413) 458-8161 (open April to Nov.)	5	sgl: $30-55 dbl: $40-65 xp: $7,g
Four Acres Motel 213 Main St., Mass. 2 Williamstown, Mass. 01267	(413) 458-8158	1	sgl: $50-65 dbl: $55-65 xp: $5
Maple Terrace Motel 555 Main St., Mass. 2 Williamstown, Mass. 01267	(413) 458-9677	2	sgl: $38-65 (B) dbl: $44-65 (B) xp: $5-10,c
The Williams Inn On The Green Williamstown, Mass. 01267	(413) 458-9371	5	sgl: $75-85 dbl: $95-120 xp: $10,c,g
The Willows Motel 480 Main St. Williamstown, Mass. 01267	(413) 458-5768	2	dbl: $42-48 xp: $5

CODES: sgl-single, **dbl**-double, **g**-group rates, **c**-special rates for children, **s**-senior citizen discount, **xp**-extra person, **MAP**-Modified American Plan, **AP**-American Plan, **B**-breakfast included, **V**-VISA, **MC**-MasterCard, **AE**-American Express, **CB**-Carte Blanche, **DC**-Diners

Credit Cards	Food	Office Open	Park While Hiking	Shuttle to Trail	Public Transportation
V/MC/AE	R-OP L	8am-10pm	Yes	Yes n/c	–
V/MC/AE D	R L	7am-11pm	Yes	–	–
V/MC/AE DC/D	R-OP L	7:30am-10pm	Yes	Yes n/c	E
V/MC/AE	R	8am-10pm	Yes	Yes n/c	E T
V/MC/AE DC/CB/D	R-OP L-OP	24 hrs.	Yes	–	E
V/MC/AE D	R L	7:30am-11pm	Yes	–	E T

Club, **AM**-Amoco, **D**-Discover, **C**-Choice, **R**-restaurant within half mile unless mileage noted, **L**-takeout lunch within half mile unless mileage noted, **OP**-on premises, **E**-public transportation to establishment, **T**-public transportation to Trail, **n/c**-no charge

Massachusetts

BED AND BREAKFASTS AND COUNTRY

Name and Address	Telephone	Miles from Trail	Rates
Canterbury Farm Fred Snow Rd. Becket, Mass. 01223	(413) 623-8765	2	dbl: $50-75 xp: $15, g
Longhouse B&B High St. Becket, Mass. 01223	(413) 623-8360	2.5	sgl: $30-45 (B) s,c,g
Dalton House 955 Main St. Dalton, Mass. 01226	(413) 684-3854	1	sgl: $43-58 (B) dbl: $58-68 (B) xp: $10,g
Bread and Roses Star Rt. 65, Box 50 Great Barrington, Mass. 01230	(413) 528-1099	7	sgl: $60 (B) dbl: $85 (B) xp: $15
Coffing-Bostwick House 98 Division St. Great Barrington, Mass. 01230	(413) 528-4511	5	sgl: $45-70 dbl: $50-75 xp: $10-35, c
Elling's B&B Guest House RD 3, Box 6, Rt. 7 Great Barrington, Mass. 01230	(413) 528-4103	3	sgl: $35-60 (B) dbl: $50-75 (B)
Greenmeadows 117 Division St. Great Barrington, Mass. 01230	(413) 528-3897	3	dbl: $60-90 xp: $20-30,g

CODES: sgl-single, **dbl**-double, **g**-group rates, **c**-special rates for children, **s**-senior citizen discount, **xp**-extra person, **MAP**-Modified American Plan, **AP**-American Plan, **B**-breakfast included, **V**-VISA, **MC**-MasterCard, **AE**-American Express, **CB**-Carte Blanche, **DC**-Diners

INNS

Credit Cards	Food	Office Open	Park While Hiking	Shuttle to Trail	Public Transportation
V/MC	R-OP L-OP	9am-9pm	Yes	–	–
V/MC	R-11 L	24 hrs.	Yes	Yes n/c	–
V/MC/AE	R L	8am-10pm	Yes	–	E T
–	R-1 L-1	24 hrs.	Yes	Yes	–
–	R-2 L-2	–	Yes	–	–
–	R L	9am-10pm	Yes	Yes	–
V/MC	R L	8am-10pm	Yes	–	E T

Club, **AM**-Amoco, **D**-Discover, **C**-Choice, **R**-restaurant within half mile unless mileage noted, **L**-takeout lunch within half mile unless mileage noted, **OP**-on premises, **E**-public transportation to establishment, **T**-public transportation to Trail, **n/c**-no charge

Massachusetts

BED AND BREAKFASTS AND COUNTRY

Name and Address	Telephone	Miles from Trail	Rates
Littlejohn Manor 1 Newsboy Monument Lane Great Barrington, Mass. 01230	(413) 528-2882	4	sgl: $45-70 (B) dbl: $50-75 (B) g
The Red Bird Inn Mass. 57 & Adsit Crosby Rd. Great Barrington, Mass. 01230	(413) 229-2433	3	sgl: $75-85 (B) dbl: $85-100 (B)
Seekonk Pines Inn 142 Seekonk Cross Rd. Great Barrington, Mass. 01230	(413) 528-4192	3.5	sgl: $45-55 (B) dbl: $65-85 (B) xp: $15,c
The Turning Point Inn RD 2, Box 140 3 Lake Buel Rd. Great Barrington, Mass. 01230	(413) 528-4777	1	sgl: $55 (B) dbl: $75-95 (B) xp: $15, c,g
Kirkmead B&B (P.O. Box 169A Stephentown, N.Y. 12168) Hancock, Mass.	(413) 738-5420	9	sgl: $35 (B) dbl: $50 (B) xp: $10,c
Mill House Inn P.O. Box 1079, Mass. 43 Hancock, Mass. 01237	(518) 733-5606 (open 11/1 to 12/15, 3/20 to 5/1)	10	sgl: $65 dbl: $75 and up xp: $15
Bascom Lodge P.O. Box 686 Lanesboro, Mass. 02137	(413) 743-1591 (open 5/15 to 10/25)	0.1	sgl: $15 c

CODES: sgl-single, **dbl**-double, **g**-group rates, **c**-special rates for children, **s**-senior citizen discount, **xp**-extra person, **MAP**-Modified American Plan, **AP**-American Plan, **B**-breakfast included, **V**-VISA, **MC**-MasterCard, **AE**-American Express, **CB**-Carte Blanche, **DC**-Diners

INNS

Credit Cards	Food	Office Open	Park While Hiking	Shuttle to Trail	Public Transportation
–	R L	6am- 11pm	–	Yes	–
–	R L-2	24 hrs.	Yes	–	–
–	R-1.5 L-1.5	8am- 9pm	Yes	Yes	–
–	R-.75 L-.75	8am- 10pm	Yes	–	–
–	R-1 L-1	8am- midnight	Yes	–	–
V/MC/AE	R L	9am- 9pm	Yes	–	–
V/MC	R-OP L-OP	6am- 10pm	Yes	–	–

Club, **AM**-Amoco, **D**-Discover, **C**-Choice, **R**-restaurant within half mile unless mileage noted, **L**-takeout lunch within half mile unless mileage noted, **OP**-on premises, **E**-public transportation to establishment, **T**-public transportation to Trail, **n/c**-no charge

Massachusetts

BED AND BREAKFASTS AND COUNTRY

Name and Address	Telephone	Miles from Trail	Rates
Townry Farm Greylock Rd. Lanesboro, Mass. 01237	(413) 443-9285	6	sgl: $30 dbl: $35 xp: $15
Chanterwood Inn Chanterwood Rd. P.O. Box 375 Lee, Mass. 01238	(413) 243-0585	4	sgl: $60-70 c
Haus Andreas Stockbridge Rd. Lee, Mass. 01238	(413) 243-3298	5	dbl: $90-225 (B)
Kingsleigh 1840 B&B 32 Park St. Lee, Mass. 01238	(413) 243-3317	2	dbl: $45-95 (B) xp: $15
Amity House 15 Cliffwood St. Lenox, Mass. 01240	(413) 637-0005 (open Jan. to Oct.)	8	sgl: $50 dbl: $60 g
Brook Farm Inn 15 Hawthorne St. Lenox, Mass. 01240	(413) 637-3013	6	sgl: $65-135 (B) dbl: $65-135 (B) xp: $15
Cornell Inn 197 Main St. Lenox, Mass. 01240	(413) 637-0562	10	dbl: $50-125 xp: $15

CODES: sgl-single, **dbl**-double, **g**-group rates, **c**-special rates for children, **s**-senior citizen discount, **xp**-extra person, **MAP**-Modified American Plan, **AP**-American Plan, **B**-breakfast included, **V**-VISA, **MC**-MasterCard, **AE**-American Express, **CB**-Carte Blanche, **DC**-Diners

INNS

Credit Cards	Food	Office Open	Park While Hiking	Shuttle to Trail	Public Transportation
–	–	9am-6:30pm	Yes	Yes	–
V/MC/AE	R-OP L-OP	7am-11pm	Yes	–	–
V/MC	R	8am-11pm	–	–	–
all major	R L	9am-10pm	Yes	Yes	E
–	R L	9am-5pm	Yes	–	E
V/MC	R L	8am-10pm	Yes	–	E
V/MC	R	8am-11pm	Yes	Yes	E

Club, **AM**-Amoco, **D**-Discover, **C**-Choice, **R**-restaurant within half mile unless mileage noted, **L**-takeout lunch within half mile unless mileage noted, **OP**-on premises, **E**-public transportation to establishment, **T**-public transportation to Trail, **n/c**-no charge

BED AND BREAKFASTS AND COUNTRY

Name and Address	Telephone	Miles from Trail	Rates
The Gables Inn 103 Walker St. Lenox, Mass. 01240	(413) 637-3416	20	dbl: $60-135 (B) xp: $20,g
Garden Gables 141 Main St. Lenox, Mass. 01240	(413) 637-0193	10	sgl: $55-125 (B) dbl: $55-125 (B) xp: $20
Underledge Inn 76 Clippwood St. Lenox, Mass. 01240	(413) 637-0236	15	dbl: $60-130 xp: $20
Walker House 74 Walker St. Lenox, Mass. 01240	(413) 637-1271	15	dbl: $45-130 xp: $15
Whistler's Inn 5 Greenwood St. Lenox, Mass. 01240	(413) 637-0975	15	sgl: $60 (B) dbl: $70-155 (B) xp: $25
Mountain Trails Mass. 23 Monterey, Mass. 01245	(413) 528-2928	0.2	sgl: $25-40 (B) dbl: $30-50 (B) xp: $10,s,c,g
Stonewood Inn S.R. 62, Box 42, Mass. 23 Monterey, Mass. 01245	(413) 269-4894	7	sgl: $65 (B) dbl: $75 (B) xp: $15,g

CODES: sgl-single, **dbl**-double, **g**-group rates, **c**-special rates for children, **s**-senior citizen discount, **xp**-extra person, **MAP**-Modified American Plan, **AP**-American Plan, **B**-breakfast included, **V**-VISA, **MC**-MasterCard, **AE**-American Express, **CB**-Carte Blanche, **DC**-Diners

INNS

Credit Cards	Food	Office Open	Park While Hiking	Shuttle to Trail	Public Transportation
V/MC/AE	R L	24 hrs.	Yes	–	E T
V/MC	R L	24 hrs.	Yes	–	E
V/MC/AE	R L	8am-11pm	Yes	–	–
–	R L	8am-midnight	Yes	–	E T
V/MC/AE	R L	7am-midnight	Yes	–	E T
–	R-3 L-OP	7am-11pm	Yes	–	–
–	R-3 L-3	24 hrs.	Yes	Yes n/c	–

Club, **AM**-Amoco, **D**-Discover, **C**-Choice, **R**-restaurant within half mile unless mileage noted, **L**-takeout lunch within half mile unless mileage noted, **OP**-on premises, **E**-public transportation to establishment, **T**-public transportation to Trail, **n/c**-no charge

Massachusetts

BED AND BREAKFASTS AND COUNTRY

Name and Address	Telephone	Miles from Trail	Rates
Chalet d'Alicia East Windsor Rd. Peru, Mass. 01235	(413) 655-8292	10	sgl: $40 (B) dbl: $45 (B)
The White Horse Inn 378 South St. Pittsfield, Mass. 01201	(413) 443-0961	8	sgl: $60-100
The Peirson Place Mass. 41 Richmond, Mass. 01254	(413) 698-2750	15	sgl: $35-60 (B) dbl: $45-145 (B) xp: $25-30,s
Daffer's Mtn. Inn Mass. 57 Sandisfield, Mass. 01255	(413) 258-4453	8	sgl: $37 dbl: $37
New Boston Inn Mass. 8 & 57, P.O. Box 120 Sandisfield, Mass. 01255	(413) 258-4477	15	dbl: $70-95 (B& B or MAP) xp: $20,g
Centuryhurst B&B Main St., U.S. 7 P.O. Box 486 Sheffield, Mass. 01257	(413) 229-8131	3	sgl: $54-58 (B) dbl: $58-62 (B)
Ivanhoe Country House Mass. 41, Undermountain Rd. Sheffield, Mass. 01257	(413) 229-2143	1	dbl: $65-89 (B) xp: $10

CODES: sgl-single, dbl-double, g-group rates, c-special rates for children, s-senior citizen discount, xp-extra person, MAP-Modified American Plan, AP-American Plan, B-breakfast included, V-VISA, MC-MasterCard, AE-American Express, CB-Carte Blanche, DC-Diners

INNS

Credit Cards	Food	Office Open	Park While Hiking	Shuttle to Trail	Public Transportation
–	R-10 L-10	9am-9pm	Yes	–	–
V/MC/AE	R-1 L-1	7am-11pm	Yes	–	E
V/MC	R	7:30am-9:30pm	Yes	–	–
V/MC	R-OP	closed Mon. and Tues.	Yes	–	–
V/MC/AE	R-OP	24 hrs.	Yes	Yes n/c	–
V/MC/AE	R L	6am-10pm	Yes	–	E
–	R-1 L-2.5	9am-11pm	Yes	Yes	–

Club, **AM**-Amoco, **D**-Discover, **C**-Choice, **R**-restaurant within half mile unless mileage noted, **L**-takeout lunch within half mile unless mileage noted, **OP**-on premises, **E**-public transportation to establishment, **T**-public transportation to Trail, **n/c**-no charge

BED AND BREAKFASTS AND COUNTRY

Name and Address	Telephone	Miles from Trail	Rates
Staveleigh House P.O. Box 608, S. Main St. Sheffield, Mass. 01257	(413) 229-2129	1	sgl: $60-70 (B) dbl: $70-85 (B)
The Egremont Inn Old Sheffield Rd. South Egremont, Mass. 01258	(413) 528-2111 (closed mid-March to end of April)	2	sgl: $50-80 dbl: $70-105 xp: $20,g
Merrell Tavern Inn Main St., Mass. 102 South Lee, Mass. 01260	(413) 243-1794	5	sgl: $55-110 dbl: $65-120 xp: $15,g
Olde Lamplighter B&B Church St. Stockbridge, Mass. 01262	(413) 298-3053	2	dbl: $50-195 (B) xp: $20,g
The Golden Goose Main Rd. Tyringham, Mass. 01264	(413) 243-3008	0.5	sgl: $50-85 dbl: $55-90
Blueberry Hill Washington Mtn. Rd. Washington, Mass. 01223	(413) 623-5859	0.5	sgl: $25 dbl: $35-50
Bucksteep Manor Washington Mtn. Rd. Washington, Mass. 01223	(413) 623-5535	1.5	sgl: $65 dbl: $70

CODES: sgl-single, **dbl**-double, **g**-group rates, **c**-special rates for children, **s**-senior citizen discount, **xp**-extra person, **MAP**-Modified American Plan, **AP**-American Plan, **B**-breakfast included, **V**-VISA, **MC**-MasterCard, **AE**-American Express, **CB**-Carte Blanche, **DC**-Diners

INNS

Credit Cards	Food	Office Open	Park While Hiking	Shuttle to Trail	Public Transportation
–	R L	8am- 8pm	Yes	Yes n/c	E
V/MC/AE	R-OP L	8am- 10pm	Yes	Yes n/c	E
V/MC/AE	R L	8am- 10pm	Yes	–	E
V/MC	R L	24 hrs.	Yes	–	E
–	–	8am- 9pm	Yes	–	–
–	R-2 L-OP	5pm- 10pm	Yes	Yes	–
V/MC	R-10 L-3	24 hrs.	Yes	–	–

Club, **AM**-Amoco, **D**-Discover, **C**-Choice, **R**-restaurant within half mile unless mileage noted, **L**-takeout lunch within half mile unless mileage noted, **OP**-on premises, **E**-public transportation to establishment, **T**-public transportation to Trail, **n/c**-no charge

Massachusetts

BED AND BREAKFASTS AND COUNTRY

Name and Address	Telephone	Miles from Trail	Rates
The Orchards Adam St. Williamstown, Mass. 01267	(413) 458-9611 (800) 231-2344 (Mass.) (800) 225-1517	2	sgl: $110-145 (MAP) dbl: $115-150 (MAP) xp: $20, s,g

CAMPGROUNDS, CABINS, AND HOSTELS

Name and Address	Telephone	Miles from Trail	Rates
Walker Island Campground Mass. 20 Chester, Mass. 01011	(413) 354-2295	12	dbl: $16-20 xp: $2-5,c,g
Chilson's Pond Camping Area Tilda Hill Rd. (North Adams, Mass. 01247) Florida, Mass.	(413) 664-6001 (open 5/10 to 10/15)	10	$8/site
Beartown State Forest P.O. Box 97, Blue Hill Rd. Monterey, Mass. 01245	(413) 528-0904	0.5	$5/site g
Prospect Lake Park Campground Prospect Lake Rd. North Egremont, Mass. 01252	(413) 528-4158	6	dbl: $16

CODES: sgl-single, **dbl**-double, **g**-group rates, **c**-special rates for children, **s**-senior citizen discount, **xp**-extra person, **MAP**-Modified American Plan, **AP**-American Plan, **B**-breakfast included, **V**-VISA, **MC**-MasterCard, **AE**-American Express, **CB**-Carte Blanche, **DC**-Diners

INNS

Credit Cards	Food	Office Open	Park While Hiking	Shuttle to Trail	Public Transportation
V/MC/AE	R-OP L-OP	24 hrs.	Yes	Yes n/c	E
–	R-1 L-OP	9am- 10pm	Yes	–	–
–	R-1.5 L-1	8am- 10pm	Yes	–	–
–	R-2.5 L-2.5	8am- midnight	Yes	–	–
V/MC	R-OP L-OP	8am- 11pm	Yes	–	–

Club, **AM**-Amoco, **D**-Discover, **C**-Choice, **R**-restaurant within half mile unless mileage noted, **L**-takeout lunch within half mile unless mileage noted, **OP**-on premises, **E**-public transportation to establishment, **T**-public transportation to Trail, **n/c**-no charge

CAMPGROUNDS, CABINS, AND HOSTEL

Name and Address	Telephone	Miles from Trail	Rates
Pine Hill Cabins 269 Cheshire Rd., Mass. 8 Pittsfield Mass. 01201	(413) 447-7214 (open 6-1 to 9-15)	5	dbl: $35 4 people: $50 xp: $7

Also see **The Peirson Place** listed under Bed and Breakfasts and Country Inns

CODES: sgl-single, **dbl**-double, **g**-group rates, **c**-special rates for children, **s**-senior citizen discount, **xp**-extra person, **MAP**-Modified American Plan, **AP**-American Plan, **B**-breakfast included, **V**-VISA, **MC**-MasterCard, **AE**-American Express, **CB**-Carte Blanche, **DC**-Diners

Credit Cards	Food	Office Open	Park While Hiking	Shuttle to Trail	Public Transportation
–	R L	6:30am-12pm	Yes	–	–

Club, **AM**-Amoco, **D**-Discover, **C**-Choice, **R**-restaurant within half mile unless mileage noted, **L**-takeout lunch within half mile unless mileage noted, **OP**-on premises, **E**-public transportation to establishment, **T**-public transportation to Trail, **n/c**-no charge

CONNECTICUT

MASSACHUSETTS-CONNECTICUT STATE LINE TO CONNECTICUT-NEW YORK STATE LINE

Appalachian Trail Guide to Massachusetts-Connecticut

The maintaining club for this area is the Connecticut Chapter of the Appalachian Mountain Club.

GETTING THERE

Air: Scheduled service is available to Hartford.
Bus: The Bonanza bus line has several runs a day between New York City and Pittsfield, Mass., stopping at Falls Village (which is on the Trail), Cornwall Bridge (about a half mile from the Trail), and Kent (about a mile from the Trail).
Taxi: Danbury, Lakeville, Litchfield, Torrington, and Winsted have taxi companies.
Hiker Shuttle Services: Jeff Daniels, 29 Old Musket Dr., Newington, Conn. 06111; Bob Hall, Macedonia Rd., Kent, Conn. 06757, (203) 927-3301 ($5 per hour, check availability).

POINTS OF INTEREST

Bear Mountain: The summit of the highest mountain entirely within the state (2,316 feet) has a monument and views of the Housatonic Valley and Berkshires. It is reached by hiking 5.5 miles north from Conn. 41, mostly at moderate grades.
Lion's Head: On the way to Bear Mountain, this site has spectacular views from its 1,738-foot summit, the southern end of the Taconic Range; a little more than two miles north from Conn. 41.
Rand's View: This is considered by many to be the finest view on the Trail in Connecticut. On a clear day, Mt. Greylock, 50 miles away in Massachusetts, is visible. The hike north from the end of Sugar Hill Road is only a little more than a mile, but there is a short, steep climb along Prospect Falls.

Housatonic River: Several times the Trail follows scenic routes along the banks of the Housatonic River, passing pine plantations, old foundations, and several brooks (see Connecticut sections 3, 4, and 6 in *Appalachian Trail Guide to Connecticut*).

ACCESS POINTS

Near Salisbury, the Trail follows Conn. 41, Lower Cobble Road, and U.S. 44 about a mile (best parking areas are at the northern and southern ends of the road walk). Near Falls Village, the Trail follows Sugar Hill Road (parking at northern end of maintained portion) and other local streets. It then crosses U.S. 7 (twice), West Cornwall Road, Conn. 4 (parking available at U.S. 7, via half-mile access trail), Guinea Road (dirt; Trail follows a short distance), River Road (which the Trail follows for several miles; only part is passable by car; parking at its northern and southern junctions with Trail), Skiff Mountain Road, and Conn. 341 (parking area). The Trail follows local roads about three miles in the Dogtail Corners area (partly in New York; best parking is near the southernmost point of the road walk, in Connecticut). The Trail also crosses Conn. 55. Most lodgings will allow patrons to park vehicles on their grounds while hiking (see the "Park While Hiking" column in the listings).

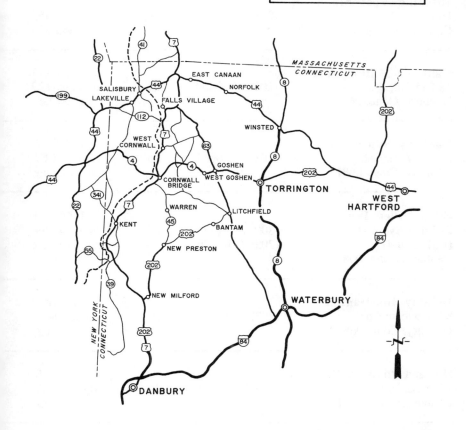
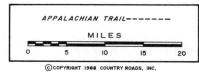

Connecticut

MOTELS AND HOTELS

Name and Address	Telephone	Miles from Trail	Rates
Hitching Post Motel U.S. 7 Cornwall Bridge, Conn. 06754	(203) 672-6219	0.25	sgl: $45-$55 dbl: $45-$55
Danbury Hilton Hotel 18 Old Ridgebury Rd. Danbury, Conn. 06810	(203) 794-0600	25	sgl: $69-117 dbl: $69-129 xp: $12,c
Danbury Super 8 Motel 3 Lake Ave. Ext. Danbury, Conn. 06811	(203) 743-0064	25	sgl: $48-64 dbl: $53-67 xp: $5,s,c,g
Ethan Allen Inn 21 Lake Ave. Ext. (I-81, Exit 4) Danbury, Conn. 06811	(800) 742-1776 (203) 744-1776	25	sgl: $80-89 dbl: $91-99 xp: $10,s,c,g
Holiday Inn-Danbury 80 Newtown Rd. Danbury, Conn. 06810	(203) 792-4000	20	sgl: $78 dbl: $84 xp: $5,s,c,g
Howard Johnson Danbury 7 N. Federal Rd. Danbury, Conn. 06810	(203) 743-6701	20	sgl: $45-70 dbl: $55-85 xp: $5,s,c,g

CODES: sgl-single, **dbl**-double, **g**-group rates, **c**-special rates for children, **s**-senior citizen discount, **xp**-extra person, **MAP**-Modified American Plan, **AP**-American Plan, **B**-breakfast included, **V**-VISA, **MC**-MasterCard, **AE**-American Express, **CB**-Carte Blanche, **DC**-Diners

Credit Cards	Food	Office Open	Park While Hiking	Shuttle to Trail	Public Transportation
V/MC/AE	R-1 L	7am-11pm	Yes	–	–
V/MC/AE DC/D	R-OP L	9am-5pm	–	–	E
V/MC/AE D	R L	24 hrs.	Yes	–	E
V/MC/AE D/DC	R-OP L-OP	24 hrs.	Yes	–	–
all major	R-OP L	24 hrs.	Yes	–	E
V/MC/AE DC/D	R-OP L-OP	24 hrs.	Yes (with permission)	–	E

Club, **AM**-Amoco, **D**-Discover, **C**-Choice, **R**-restaurant within half mile unless mileage noted, **L**-takeout lunch within half mile unless mileage noted, **OP**-on premises, **E**-public transportation to establishment, **T**-public transportation to Trail, **n/c**-no charge

MOTELS AND HOTELS

Name and Address	Telephone	Miles from Trail	Rates
Village Coffee Shop (Motel) U.S. 7 Falls Village, Conn. 06031	(203) 824-7886 (open May to mid-Oct.)	0.25	dbl: $45
Iron Masters Motor Inn Main St., Conn. 44 & 41 Lakeville, Conn. 06039	(203) 435-9844	1	sgl: $52-85 dbl: $65-85 xp: $6,c
Connecticut Maple Leaf Motor Lodge Rt. 2, 244 Kent Rd. New Milford, Conn. 06776	(203) 354-2633	10	sgl: $36-60 dbl: $45-67 xp: $3-10,s,g

BED AND BREAKFASTS AND COUNTRY

Name and Address	Telephone	Miles from Trail	Rates
Birches Inn Westshore Rd. (on Lake Waramaug) New Preston, Conn. 06777	(203) 868-0229	20	sgl: $58-78 dbl: $68-88 xp: $10,s,c,g
Hopkins Inn Hopkins Rd. New Preston, Conn. 06777	(203) 868-7295 (open April to Dec.)	10	dbl: $45-61 xp: $5
Manor House Maple Ave., P.O. Box 447 Norfolk, Conn. 06058	(203) 542-5690	10	sgl: $45-135 (B) dbl: $55-135 (B) xp: $20,s

CODES: sgl-single, **dbl**-double, **g**-group rates, **c**-special rates for children, **s**-senior citizen discount, **xp**-extra person, **MAP**-Modified American Plan, **AP**-American Plan, **B**-breakfast included, **V**-VISA, **MC**-MasterCard, **AE**-American Express, **CB**-Carte Blanche, **DC**-Diners

Credit Cards	Food	Office Open	Park While Hiking	Shuttle to Trail	Public Transportation
V/MC	R-OP L-OP	varies	Yes	–	E
V/MC/AE DC	R-OP L	7am-11pm	Yes	Yes n/c	–
V/MC/AE	R L-OP	24 hrs.	Yes	–	E T

INNS

V/MC	R-OP L-OP	24 hrs.	Yes	–	E T
–	R-OP L-3	8am-11pm	Yes	–	–
V/MC/AE	R L	10am-8pm	Yes	Yes	E

Club, **AM**-Amoco, **D**-Discover, **C**-Choice, **R**-restaurant within half mile unless mileage noted, **L**-takeout lunch within half mile unless mileage noted, **OP**-on premises, **E**-public transportation to establishment, **T**-public transportation to Trail, **n/c**-no charge

BED AND BREAKFAST AND COUNTRY

Name and Address	Telephone	Miles from Trail	Rates
Mountain Views Inn Conn. 272, P.O. Box 467 Norfolk, Conn. 06058	(203) 542-5595 (closed in March)	15	dbl: $50-100 xp: $10
Under Mountain Inn Undermountain Rd. Salisbury, Conn. 06068	(203) 435-0242 (closed mid-Dec., mid-March to mid-April)	0.7	sgl: $85-113 (MAP) dbl: $120-150 (MAP) xp: $40-50
Yesterday's Yankee B&B U.S. 44 East Salisbury, Conn. 06068	(203) 435-9539	0.25	dbl: $60-70 (B) xp: $20
Turning Point Farm Rt. 45, Cornwall Bridge Warren, Conn. 06754	(203) 868-7775	4	sgl: $65 dbl: $75 xp: $45
Hilltop Haven Dibble Hill Rd. West Cornwall, Conn. 06796	(203) 672-6871 reserv. only	5	dbl: $95 (B) 2-night min.
Provincial House 151 Main St. Winsted, Conn. 06098	(203) 379-1631	20	sgl: $35-75 (B) xp: $10,s

CODES: sgl-single, **dbl**-double, **g**-group rates, **c**-special rates for children, **s**-senior citizen discount, **xp**-extra person, **MAP**-Modified American Plan, **AP**-American Plan, **B**-breakfast included, **V**-VISA, **MC**-MasterCard, **AE**-American Express, **CB**-Carte Blanche, **DC**-Diners

INNS

Credit Cards	Food	Office Open	Park While Hiking	Shuttle to Trail	Public Transportation
V/MC	R	8am-10pm	Yes	–	–
V/MC/AE	R-OP	2pm-7pm	Yes	–	–
V/MC/AE	R L	8am-9pm	Yes	Yes n/c	E
–	R-1 L-1	24 hrs.	Yes	–	–
–	R-1.5 L-1.5	24 hrs.	Yes	Yes	–
V/MC	R L	8am-10pm	Yes	–	E

Club, **AM**-Amoco, **D**-Discover, **C**-Choice, **R**-restaurant within half mile unless mileage noted, **L**-takeout lunch within half mile unless mileage noted, **OP**-on premises, **E**-public transportation to establishment, **T**-public transportation to Trail, **n/c**-no charge

Connecticut

CAMPGROUNDS, CABINS, AND HOSTELS

Name and Address	Telephone	Miles from Trail	Rates
Housatonic Meadows State Park U.S. 7 Cornwall Bridge, Conn. 06754	(203) 672-6772 (open 4/15 to 1/1)	1	$7/site
Lone Oak Campsites U.S. 44 East Canaan, Conn. 06024	(800) 422-CAMP (203) 824-7051 (open 4/15 to 10/15)	11	$15/family s,g
Mohawk Campground P.O. Box 488, Conn. 4 W. Goshen, Conn. 06756	(203) 491-2231 (open 5/6 to 10/1)	0.25	dbl: $17 xp: $3,g

CODES: sgl-single, **dbl**-double, **g**-group rates, **c**-special rates for children, **s**-senior citizen discount, **xp**-extra person, **MAP**-Modified American Plan, **AP**-American Plan, **B**-breakfast included, **V**-VISA, **MC**-MasterCard, **AE**-American Express, **CB**-Carte Blanche, **DC**-Diners

Credit Cards	Food	Office Open	Park While Hiking	Shuttle to Trail	Public Transportation
–	R L	evenings and weekends	–	–	–
V/MC	R-4.5 L-4.5	8am-9pm	Yes	–	–
–	R-8 L-4	9am-9pm	Yes	–	–

Club, **AM**-Amoco, **D**-Discover, **C**-Choice, **R**-restaurant within half mile unless mileage noted, **L**-takeout lunch within half mile unless mileage noted, **OP**-on premises, **E**-public transportation to establishment, **T**-public transportation to Trail, **n/c**-no charge